RACHAEL BROWNELL

MOMMY DOESN'T DRINK HERE ANYMORE

GETTING THROUGH THE FIRST YEAR OF SOBRIETY

Conari Press

contents

PART I

away

PART II

toward recovery

PART III

first year of sobriety

preface

My name is Rachael and I couldn't possibly be an alcoholic. I am a well-educated, reasonably well-adjusted, thirty-nine-year-old woman with a home and a family, children, a good job, and ambition. I drink sometimes to unwind and to give myself a treat after a long day shuttling kids, working, making dinner, folding laundry, and sweeping floors, but I keep it under control. I manage all right.

I am on the cusp of middle age, with the usual questions about the meaning of life and how to balance work and children. I wonder how it has happened that my friends and I have become mothers; we used to be English and Politics majors, clasping Edith Wharton and French feminist theory to our chests as we ran across campus to meet our lovers. We used to think we could do anything with enough hard work and smarts.

This confidence has only now started to rub off, but I figure it's par for the course and about time anyway. My college roommate and I reminisce about those bygone days. We laugh about how quickly twenty years flew by.

I am not an alcoholic. And yet, I love to drink. I am in love with drinking. And I have absolutely no idea how this has happened. I am scared that something is falling away.

My heart? My drive? My joy?

Praise for
Mommy Doesn't Drink Here Anymore

"Brownell's evocative and poignant *Mommy Doesn't Drink
Here Anymore* is the story of every woman, a redemptive
coming of age memoir as challenging as it is healing;
a support group in prose. A triumph for all women."
—Rebecca Woolf, author of *Rockabye: From Wild to Child*

"Rachael Brownell's true story of her journey into those
first 12 months of recovery is a candid mirror. Written
straight from her heart, Brownell understands the denial,
fear, guilt and shame. She also conveys the pride she
gained as she continued in her recovery. Comfort, encour-
agement and support are interwoven with her words. A
gift for anyone who is seeking their own Truth regarding
addiction and recovery." —Barbara Joy, author of *Easy Does
It, Mom*

"*Mommy Doesn't Drink Here Anymore* is an excellent read. I
was absolutely entranced by Brownell's journey, her wit,
her honesty, her special connection to Ted (her recovery
soul mate), and the many women who helped her stay
sober. And I was so relieved that she got the message. Her
story touched me deeply, not just because I am a woman in
recovery, but because a story of hope resonates. This book
deserves a wide audience." —Karen Casey, Ph.D., author
of *Each Day a New Beginning* and *Change Your Mind and
Your Life Will Follow*

Mommy Doesn't Drink Here Anymore not only gives readers
insight into the effects of addiction on the entire family,
but solutions for those in the grips of family trauma.
Rachael's journey, well written with wit, humor, and
brutal honesty, is a must-read." —Barb Rogers, author of
Twenty-Five Words and *Keep It Simple and Sane*

MOMMY
DOESN'T
DRINK
HERE
ANYMORE

To Tony

Keep Rocking Reevey / dude

First published in 2009 by Conari Press,
an imprint of Red Wheel/Weiser, LLC
With offices at:
500 Third Street, Suite 230
San Francisco, CA 94107
www.redwheelweiser.com

ISBN: 978-1-57324-409-1
Library of Congress Cataloging-in-Publication Data is available
upon request.

Cover and text design by Sara Gillingham.
Typeset in Hoefler Text and Knockout.
Cover and interior illustrations © Sara Gillingham, 2009

Printed in Canada
TCP
10 9 8 7 6 5 4 3 2 1

I learn later that alcohol abuse is a symptom of a greater disease, a spiritual disease that renders us incapable of accessing our better, more loving selves. This certainly was the case for me and for many others like me.

Who Should Read This Book

I'm not here to tell you that you're an alcoholic and that you're doing your life all wrong. I'm not here to tell you that you should take better care of yourself, run 4 miles a day, give up expensive shoes and crazy lovin', or that you'll lose everything if you keep up with the bad actions and the hooch and the swearing. I'm also not here to tell you that you are a bad mother or father if you need alcohol to get you through those long hard evening hours, or that in your secret heart you sometimes wonder where your life went. Believe me, I truly understand.

I am here to tell you that you and I are more alike than you might first believe. I am at your PTA meetings and your place of work, bagging your groceries, making your latte, caring for your parents, cleaning your carpets, writing your legal documents, and planning your retirement. In offices and Laundromats and kitchens across the land, I and others like me often suffer in silence, believing that if we come forward we'll be shunned, shamed, and judged. We often fear there is no safe haven and nowhere to turn but toward a glass of booze (or ten) or a line or some pills. We believe that to drink or use makes the best sense given what we've been through; that we're justified in our actions and you couldn't possibly understand.

We, addicts and alcoholics, often live in a world of quiet misery and shame, particularly if we're parents, and we often wonder whether we should end it all and save ourselves and others the unnecessary misery of knowing us. We are people like you, but in the extreme.

We harbor secret dreams and desires. We shut ourselves off from judgment and risk. We use alcohol or drugs to kill the pain. We might drink for years "normally," able to put it aside for months at a time, but then something will shift and all of a sudden we need alcohol to do our lives. It will happen gradually and we might not even notice. But the signs are there: bottles hidden around and horded, daily hangovers, an inability to stop at just one drink, an increasing irritability or depression, and an unwillingness to stop.

But you don't have to have a problem with alcohol (or anything at all) to read this book. You can be the happiest, most well-adjusted person on the planet, with taut thighs, low blood pressure, and a daily yoga practice, with not a care in the world. Even you might enjoy this book.

You might get something out of this book if:

★ You are an adult child of an alcoholic.
★ You fear your significant other might have a problem with drugs and/or alcohol.
★ You love someone who is in recovery or who you think drinks too much.
★ You look good on the outside, but feel utterly miserable and lost on the inside.
★ You drink or use drugs a little more than you think you should.
★ You like to hear about people who make bigger mistakes than you'd ever dream of making in your own life.

acknowledgments

This book would not exist without Amber (who had the idea in the first place) and the wonderful people at Red Wheel/Weiser and Conari Press who strive to make the world better through the published word. This book would not be possible without the loving support of my brothers, my parents, my husband, and my children.

I owe a debt of undying gratitude to the people in my home group, who loved me when I could not love myself, who generously shared their stories, their bad coffee, and their time. Particular thanks to Diana, Vida, and Paul. Thanks also especially to Jill, who saved me from myself and helped me laugh during those first 30 days, and to Carla, without whom this first year would have been much less rich.

To the inspiring writers who keep my brain firing: Anne Lamott, Ann Patchett, Rebecca Woolf and Hollis Gillespie. To David Sheff, whose stunning book about his son's drug abuse helped me understand what it's like to be on the other side of addiction.

To Michelle and Paige, who slogged through the early drafts. To Diane and Michelle, whose friendships have been a great joy for more than twenty years.

To Josephine, Olivia, and Violet, my three true loves, the apples of my eye.

Mommy Doesn't Drink Here Anymore

To Mom, who showed me the way. To Barb and Dad, who helped me through that first Christmas and many, many days since. To Mark and Loren, my brotherly pillars of strength and love, without whom my life would have been inordinately less beautiful and far less funny. To the countless people who have gone before and paved the way for those of us who reach out for help with our addiction and find it, one day at a time.

And to Brian, who already knows about love and devotion and who will always be my friend.

introduction
Mommy Needs Many Drinks

It is a sunny spring afternoon and the video captures our three little girls playing outside in the big plastic pool, sliding down the orange slide, squealing with delight and denying they're cold, despite blue lips and shivers. They seem so small and fragile when I look at them in pictures or home movies, but on this warm, bright afternoon they fill up the inside of my brain with shrieks of joy and delight. I don't take my eyes off of them, nor do I put down my glass of white wine. In the video, I'm in and out of frame, helping our youngest into her life vest, assisting the older girls with swimsuits and towels, looking away from the camera, always with a drink in my hand. It's a jelly glass, the kind some people use for juice, with only a splash of white wine left in the bottom. I hold on to it despite the juggling act this requires. Like a one-handed circus act, I fasten Velcro, lift 30 pounds of child, and bend to remove a spider from the pool.

If I close my eyes now, more than a year later, I remember other things about that day.

The wine is from a huge box they've started selling next to the flower arrangements and balloons at the grocery store down the hill. With its easy-pour spout and sweet wine that tastes like soda pop, it's easy to ignore that it holds about two and a half bottles of wine and that I can put away one of those boxes in two days or less. I explain it away as a lark; something fun to spice up a family afternoon at home. If it's after 4 P.M., I've already had two or three glasses and I'm warm and cheerful. I'm more than happy to make dinner, assist little swimmers, and make funny asides to the camera—to accommodate the seemingly endless needs of our small children. How I drink isn't that different from many of my friends. What is starting to be different is how my day begins to revolve around it. I'm a little planet, and crisp white wine is my sun.

And I like to believe that no one notices. I usually don't drive anywhere, I mostly don't make any calls, and no one ever asks why I drink so much, mostly because I lie when they do. I intentionally do not count the growing number of refills each afternoon and evening, but one or two is becoming four or five more and more frequently.

It's not really a problem.
Plenty of parents drink.

I think this secretly, but I never look at the camera and I do not look into my husband's eyes. I look down and away, keep myself moving and only vaguely present, my body an apparition held aloft from reality by a river of white wine.

In the video, as in most of my drinking evenings, I'm happy for a while, a traveler on a road leading away from this place. Drinking gives me patience for the tasks at hand: repetitive conversations with young children, dishes, diapers, bills, and discipline. I grew up with an alcoholic, and I've learned to keep my ears tuned to drinking trouble in others, yet I remain stubbornly oblivious to my own. There is always a know-it-all voice inside my brain: *You drink an awful lot like an alcoholic,* but it's the same voice that tells me I should run every morning, eat tofu, and wear a size 4, so I feel justified in paying it little mind.

Killjoy inner voice. Who needs you anyway?

As well as Mommy's Little Daily Vacation, drinking is also my muse. Hired to write for Babble.com, an online magazine for a "new generation of parents," I now have another excuse to pour the wine. Booze fuels my snarky rejection of sunny assumptions about mothers portrayed in mainstream media. On Babble's Strollerderby blog I write about sex, kid-free vacations, divorce, and other previously taboo topics. Getting loose makes writing feel rebellious and assures me I'm part of a revolution, where we talk and write about our kids but aren't afraid to assert our artistic, sexual, authentic selves over the din of our old lives falling away.

Add to this the proliferation of memoirs addressing the existential challenges of modern parenthood, and it's clear that this revolution is happening in text as well as online. Many of these writer-parents share breadwinning and childrearing and are interested in raising well-loved and well-adjusted children but are also rebels with a deep-seated longing for self-expression. I count myself among this group. We may be confused and narcissistic, but we are also on to something.

Mommy Doesn't Drink Here Anymore

From books like Rebecca Woolf's *Rockabye: From Wild to Child* to blogs like Jessica Ashley's *Sassafrass,* descriptions of transforming oneself from an individual to a parent are everywhere. The subtext (because in my generation—X—there is *always* a subtext) to all this jawing and writing and confessing is that parenting is hard and we're not afraid to talk about it. The conversation can be predictable (having a baby is hard), but also transformative (How can you recapture your sexual self after having kids?). And for many of us, our real or imagined inability to fit into the neighborhood playgroup makes virtual socializing more crucial than ever.

It may seem overly simplistic to think reading, writing, blogging about the necessity of cocktail playdates substantiates our claims that we're happy, free, and unconventional, but it works for me, and I suspect for many others. Even though true addiction has nothing to do with intellectual proclivities, social movements, or parenting philosophies, I've since learned that the disease is latent in many of us, just waiting for any old excuse to rage across our lives.

For me, that excuse is motherhood.

I like to joke that life without alcohol isn't worth living. I say it in jest, but I am speaking in code, looking for other parents who laugh with me, then nod and say, "Can I get you another?" I can easily identify my type of people by whether they drink (relaxed like me) or not (too serious). I keep the conversation light, but drinking is the crux of the matter, the primary purpose for any gathering, not kids and not husbands or work. There are books everywhere agreeing with me—blogs with cocktails, martinis, and headaches in their titles—all signs suggesting I am part of a swift current of parents who know not to take it all too hard. Where a prior generation said, "Never trust anyone over thirty," I secretly believe, "Never trust a mother who doesn't drink."

It is cute and clever.

It is killing me.

When I decide to sober up, I have three children five years and younger, a house, a job, and a second husband. Their care and well-being keeps me committed and clear in my intention to stay sober in the face of all of the great reasons to keep drinking. On the other hand, getting sober while parenting young children is torture. No matter how exhausted, sick, confused, and emotional I feel, the kids count on me to make lunches, do laundry, and provide love, hugs, and kisses. Since I choose not to go to treatment, they get front row seats into those first months of hell. Poor kids.

Furthermore, when I awaken from my alcohol-induced five-year slumber, I am not the same person; and neither are they. As we all find out, the road to recovery from alcoholism is long and arduous and never ending. Add in the task of parenting and figuring out life as a sober adult, and the whole thing gets interesting fast.

Of course, many parents manage with far more equanimity and grace than I possess to find a way through new parenthood with enough built-in health and support to get by. It didn't happen that way for me. Motherhood sent me on a journey, equal parts self-discovery and self-destruction. Whether wrought from stubbornness or a proclivity toward addiction, motherhood sent me into full-blown alcoholism and nearly toppled everything dear to me in five short years.

The transition to parenthood—the letting go of self, the deep responsibility for another human being, the occasional despair when encountering the tectonic shifts parenting requires—amplifies the best and the worst in each of us. For those with potential drug or alcohol problems, these challenges are compounded by fuzzy thinking, addiction, and an obsession with obliterating reality. We might tell ourselves that we're just having fun and cutting loose after long hours at the beck and call of wee dictators. We might tell ourselves anything just to keep up the façade of keeping it all together. But the truth is, we drink because we must.

This is my story. Maybe it's yours too.

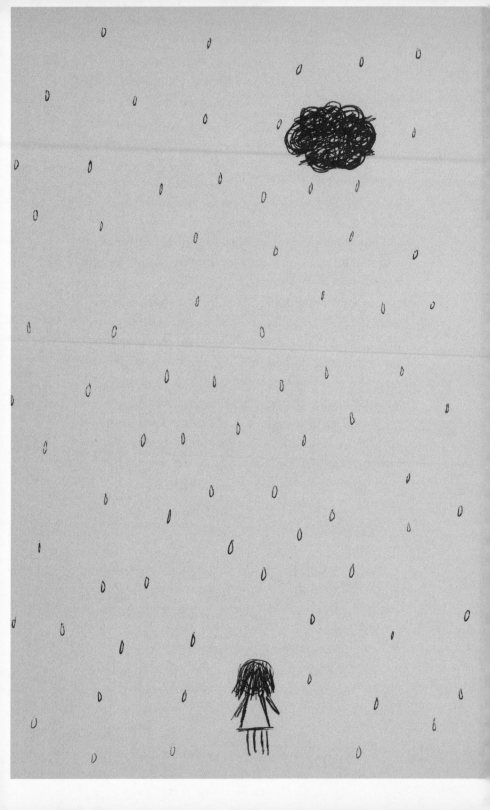

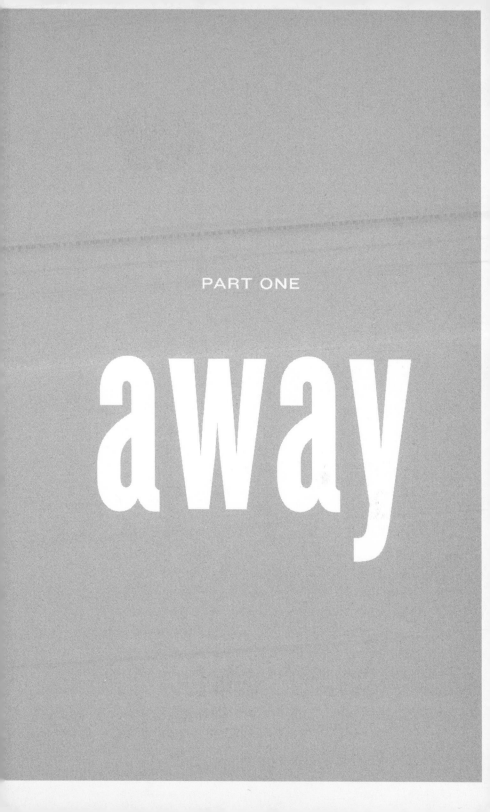

PART ONE

away

CHAPTER 1

before . . .

I am a ten-year-old bookworm of a girl, living in a
cozy house on the edge of a forest of tall evergreens
that slope down a hill just beyond my back yard. As
you enter the woods, you can easily imagine that
you're all alone and free. It is exciting to have adven-
tures this close to home, safe but distant. My two
brothers and I dominate our domain with wild calls
and double dares. We climb trees and look for bugs
and whoop and holler and act tough. These are the
happiest days of my childhood.

And they are numbered.

My room is across from my brothers' on the
top floor of the house. My mom and I had recently
hung pink, white, and blue flowered curtains with a
matching bedspread and pillow shams from Sears.
My beautiful room is so pretty and quiet; snug, cozy,
and warm. There are shelves against the far wall that
display my dolls and books and a funny old jewelry
box from my grandmother. My very own room! And
even though I hang the "No Boys Allowed" sign, I
always relent and let my brothers in. They are my best
playmates, even when they refuse to follow orders. I
like to sit on the floor near the window overlooking
our woods and write in my diary. Sometimes I write
about how I drink wine like Mom (it isn't true,
but it's fun to pretend) and about the birds I see in
the woods behind our house.

One afternoon, my brothers and I sneak onto
the roof from my window. Sitting up there with
them is forbidden, and I feel a thrilling lurch in

Mommy Doesn't Drink Here Anymore

my stomach as I climb out to see all there is to see. We're only two stories up from the ground, but we can see the Puget Sound over the tops of our trees and the distant mountains, with the clear eyes of well-loved children.

Downstairs our parents are arguing again, and there is a dark cloud over our home; increasingly our outdoor play is more escape than idyll.

"I can't do this anymore, Ken." Mom's voice carries up to our far-viewing perch.

"You can't just decide to break up our family," Dad pleads.

"I don't know what to do. . . . I'm so unhappy," Mom cries.

My brothers and I walk downstairs and I make my way over to the couch. I rub Mom's back and look over at Dad, who is coughing a lot and swallowing repeatedly.

I'm going to live here forever with my family.

I don't actually think that. I take it for granted, like my next breath full of sufficient oxygen, like my mother and father who love me.

One morning I come into the kitchen and see my mother riffling around in the bottom drawer of the refrigerator. She is wearing her blue-and-white night-gown, and her back is to me.

"Hi Mom," I say.

She jumps a mile and closes the door quickly. "Good morning, honey!"

She reaches to give me a hug and holds me close. My eyes wander to the fridge, and I wrestle away and open the door. My eyes scan quickly to find the bottle in the crisper. When I look at her, she rushes to explain, "I'm sorry. I didn't want you to see. I just have a little wine in there, but I'm trying to stop. Mommy is trying to stop drinking." And then she cries.

"Mom. Just stop. Just stop," I beg.

She says, "I'll try."

And she does for a while.

At recess one morning, I hear a siren and my stomach drops. I know the ambulance is going to our house. I know it's sounding a call of alarm for my mother.

"I know it is for Mommy!" I insist to my older brother, pulling on his arm while trying to convince him to leave school with me to walk home, but he shrugs me off.

I can't listen as my teacher explains how we'll be starting a school newspaper soon, and each of us will have a chance to write an article. I want to be a writer, but all I can think is:

I need to go home right now!

Finally school ends, and when we arrive home, Mom is there. She's sick on the couch with the shades drawn. The ambulance was called for her. I was right!

"Mom, what happened?" I demand.

She smiles and says in her high, weak voice, "Oh honey, don't worry, Mommy just took some pills that didn't mix with wine, and they needed to give me something to feel better."

I sit and pet her hair. She asks if I'll rub her back and sit by her for a while.

It is dark in our small house, but cozy and warm. I can't go upstairs to my room or outside to play because I'm afraid if I leave her she'll die. I don't remember where the rest of my family is. . . . I just remember if I hold her hand and pet her head, I can make it all right.

Later that evening, my dad is making hamburgers in the kitchen. The smells of dinner are comforting, as if all we need to do is sit together around the table and everything will be just fine.

My brothers are in the family room, watching TV on their stomachs, with their chins resting on their hands. They are two in a row, and I fit right on the end.

We have a song we sing when we walk around the house together.

> *We are pals*
> *We are pals*
> *We are the best ones*
> *We are the strong ones*

I sing it to myself as I lie down next to my little brother, who turns and asks me to quiet down so he can hear the TV (he and my older brother are watching a show from the 1970s called *Kids Are People Too*).

A few weeks later, my parents call a family meeting. I sit on my dad's lap in his black chair. Over the top of the chair is a hanging lamp from a kit, and my elevation brings the lightbulb to rest on the top of my head. It's warm under there and the light makes it hard to see the others gathered around. Mom says that they have decided to separate for a while. We'll move away with her, and Dad will stay here.

My dad starts to cry and says, "This is a helluva way to keep a family together." My parents have separated before. When we were very young, we moved to another town for a while. This house with my very own room was our new beginning. This was our family staying together.

I squint at my mom, sitting in shadow against the window. She's using that fake high voice again. "Everything will be fine. Your father and I will always love you." Huh? She might as well have said, "You will always have a head." Reassurances like this make me incredibly nervous even still.

I take my younger brother's hand, and we walk upstairs. My older brother follows behind.

We are pals.

I hope that Mom will change her mind, but a few weeks later she takes me on a ferry ride across the Sound and tells me they're divorcing. I shake my head because I don't think I've heard her clearly. She tells me this is for the best, and I want my parents to be happy, right?

As she talks, it feels as if the ferryboat is tipping over. I look out the window and imagine the water is coming up toward me.

Mommy Doesn't Drink Here Anymore

I still have this dream thirty years later. I am in a building or on a boat, and it starts to tip and I watch helplessly as the water rises toward me. I know I'm going to drown, and there is nothing I can do to prevent it. It is completely out of my control.

We move into an apartment complex called Lynnwood Garden Village. It is neither a garden nor a village, but the place is snug and there is a pool. The other kids seem wild, and my mom is on the phone every night crying and telling us to keep it down. We have left our house near the woods. I don't live in my blue room anymore. My family is broken. And I feel so sad I can barely speak. I hold my younger brother's hand as we walk to the grocery store across the street for milk or eggs or to get out of the house. He's small and blond and my little baby boy.

I'm his mama.

I say this to myself and somehow it makes me feel better and stronger. I might tell him that I'm his real mama. I can't remember.

We go to visit Dad at the house. I walk up to my room. The curtains have been taken down; the bed is gone, as are all my things. The shelves are empty except for a few boxes, and I sit on the blue carpet. Everything matches here, but everything is gone.

My dad comes upstairs to find me. "Rachael, we can decorate your room again. Would you like that? Would you like to put some of your things in here? This can still be your place." This isn't my place anymore.

I look at him and say nothing. Saying nothing is a new power I have. It makes adults uncomfortable, and for a minute makes me feel like I might know what to do or say next to fix it. When I say nothing, I'm powerful. He asks again, "Rachael? How are you doing, hon?"

I turn my head away and fight off the tears. "I'm fine, Dad. Fine. You and Mom will be happier this way, and we'll get used to it. I don't want to put my things in here. This isn't my room anymore."

He's hurt and surprised. "Sometimes you're hard as nails, Rachael," and he turns and walks back down the stairs.

We return to the apartment. Mom takes us to some 12-Step meetings. We don't like them very much. People smoke and swear and stare at us. My mom wants us to know what she's trying to do. All I know is that I'm angry and quiet and that I don't trust her. I love her and protect her, but she's unpredictable. My brothers and I stop fighting and start sleeping together in my oldest brother's bed. I remember feeling that if I burrow far enough into my older brother's bony shoulder, I can escape this big huge sadness.

It is the first day of sixth grade, and I'm standing at the edge of the field. There are three girls jumping rope, and I can see my older brother off in the distance with the other boys, playing baseball. I stand on one leg. I stand on the other. I see Kathy over there and I wave. She looks up at me, smiles, and then whispers into another girl's ear. I go to Kathy's house in the mornings before school. She and her sister are asleep, and I can stay at their house and sit downstairs as long as I'm quiet. My mom drops me there because she works full time now, for the first time since I was born. Everyone knows my family is broken. Kathy's mom is uncomfortable around me, and Kathy and her sister look at me like I'm a stray and they need to be careful or I'll bite them. I've never felt this out of place in my life. Their mom makes them breakfast while I watch TV. I try not to move or make a sound.

I know that Kathy has told the other kids my parents are getting a divorce. We used to be friends, but now she seems embarrassed by me. I'm sure that my broken family shows through my skin, hanging over me like a neon sign. And I have nowhere to hide.

CHAPTER 2

oh mama

It's my thirty-second birthday, and my friend Anna and I are throwing a combined birthday/housewarming party. We're both recently divorced. My marriage, to a nice Canadian man, didn't last long, but since we didn't have kids and ended friends, the whole thing seemed harmless enough.

Anna and I are thrilled to have an excuse to gather friends together to drink to our new freedom. We have buckets of margarita mix, wine, beer, and an ice chest full of mixers and hard lemonade. The house is an amazing summer rental in a nice neighborhood in Seattle. It has a wonderful backyard filled with roses, begonias, and rhododendrons. Everything is blooming, and anything seems possible. We are young and free.

At the bottom of the yard is a wooden bench underneath a trellis with trailing clematis. We hang white lights around the trellis so that the bench is softly lit, all ready for a great romantic scene.

As people begin pouring in, my friend Shannon pulls me aside.

"So I hope you don't get mad at me, Rachael."

"Why would I be mad?"

"Well, see, I sort of invited someone. Someone I think you might like."

"But Shannon, I already have a date, he's over there dancing." And then, curious, "So who did you invite?"

"Oh just someone I met a few weeks ago. He's a single dad. Very handsome. I think you'll like him."

And right on cue, I see him walk into the party and look around.

Mommy Doesn't Drink Here Anymore

He's very good looking, medium build, with dark brown hair and shocking dark blue eyes. He's asking someone where the birthday girl is and spots Shannon and me across the patio.

He introduces himself, thanks me for the invitation, and offers me a small pretty bag with a bow.

"My daughter helped me pick this out. I hope you like bath things." He smiles widely and says, "Happy birthday, Rachael."

Happy birthday to me!

We sit and talk all evening underneath the white lights of the trellis. I have several margaritas during our discussion, and each leaves me warmer than the last.

At the end of the evening, he takes my hand and kisses it. "I want to see you again, Rachael." And I can do nothing but nod my agreement. This man is so beautiful, he hurts my eyes.

We move in together three months later. My dad expresses concern at the rapid pace of this new relationship, hatched only six months after my divorce, but I assure him that all is well. I totally trust Jon.

"Nothing to worry about, Dad," I chirp as we drive to the store.

He looks doubtful but says nothing further.

I'm sure that anyone near Jon can't help falling in love. He is so attractive that all people stand helplessly by, drawn into his aura. Gay, straight, man, woman—doesn't matter. They're all powerless over his allure.

The Christmas after moving in together, Jon and I host a small gift exchange with his family. Everyone sits on the floor of our small apartment, and he rubs my back as I lean into him. At one point, he puts on Dean Martin's "Return to Me," and we dance in the middle of the circle, leaning into each other. That Christmas I give him an engraved watch: "To my one true love."

I have never been this in love. Nor have I ever had this much to lose.

About five months into our relationship, I am pregnant. It isn't planned, but he and I are thrilled. This assuages my fear of abandonment for a while, but then I get large and grumpy and trapped, trapped in a body over which I have no control.

The twins are born on December 11, 2001. We schedule the induction after my obstetrician takes pity on me (short people should not be allowed to carry twins). They arrive after a reasonably short labor and well-administered epidural. Twelve hours start to finish. Jon is a champ in the delivery room, coaching me, counting loudly, and whispering into my ear, "I'm proud of you, Rachael."

We each hold a twin as the nurse snaps a picture before whisking the babies away for a quick check. I cannot believe these lovely butterflies, these kittens, these humans are mine.

Jon and I have made two people—two permanent people—together. Our love is out in the world now for all to see. And now I have something to hold on to

Mommy Doesn't Drink Here Anymore

to prove we'll stay together, people to love unreservedly: our baby daughters.

The nurse recommends we put the twins in the nursery so we can catch a few hours of sleep before "it all begins." I remember the darkened room, the nurse wheeling the teeny tiny twins away and feeling a sharp pain of separation in my stomach. Jon quickly falls asleep on the couch next to me, but about 10 minutes later, I start worrying about the twins, and I ask Jon to get the nurse and bring the twins back to me.

When they are wheeled back into the dark room, I lean up on an elbow so I can look into their crib. They are so tiny, and they wear little hats. I sleep with my hand resting on the crib mattress. I wake every few minutes to make sure they're breathing, and then I fall back asleep.

I remember looking in the mirror the next day and hopping up and down because I weigh 50 pounds less, practically sylphlike compared to my body two days before. How lovely to walk again without hefting around 50 pounds of baby! Not long after, the fatigue kicks in as we negotiate the necessary forms and vaccinations before the hospital will release us.

We fasten the twins into the backseat of Jon's gray sedan. The babies are fussy but also very sleepy, and I sit in between them in the back so I can watch them while Jon drives us home. Home for the first few months after the twins are born will be my dad and stepmom's house. Jon and I have read too many books about the realities of life after twins and decide that more rather than less support is essential. As it turns out, this is a very wise move.

Jon starts the car and locks the doors. As the locks click into place, I feel safe and comfortable. I am happy in the back looking at our babies and leaning into the cushy seats while I listen to them breathe.

"Holy shit! Rach! Look!" Jon slams on the brakes and points in front of us.

I lean forward and see a woman running across the road screaming, "No no nooooooooo!" . . . In the middle of the road in front of us, a burgundy van sits diagonally blocking traffic. I look at the van more closely and see a body sticking out from under the back tire. Next to the body is a motorcycle tipped over on its side. The screaming woman kneels by the body and yells, "Somebody help!"

I hold my hands over my eyes and yell, "Jon! Call 9-1-1!"

He dials up and reports what we've seen.

My stomach drops to the floor, and I feel like I've not eaten or slept in years. . . . The babies are still sleeping, but I'm holding on to my seat so tightly my knuckles are turning white.

Life is bigger than I ever imagined, and I am smaller. Is the keening woman the motorcyclist's mother? Is she his girlfriend? What if she's pregnant with his baby? What if he is the person she loves most in the whole world and now he's gone?

Mommy Doesn't Drink Here Anymore

I am suddenly vulnerable to attack from all sides. If someone holds a needle to my baby's foot to administer a vaccine and I nearly fall to the floor in hysterics, I know I will not survive their inevitable motorcycle accident. I won't be keening and crying; I'll be eviscerated. Murdered.

After the police and the ambulance arrive, we start off again for my parents' house. We arrive home and carry the babies to our room in the front of the house. Thank God for home. We've set up our furniture in two front rooms in my parent's house. We place the twins, still sleeping, on top of our green bedspread, and I kick off my shoes and enjoy the feel of the knobby wool carpet against my swollen feet. The room feels very cold, and I cover the twins with blankets and secure their hats. I pull up a chair and sit and watch, enjoying their peaceful beauty, but also holding my breath and repeating a prayer of protection.

Later, after a foiled attempt at nursing the twins, I call for Jon and find him in the living room reading a book. He looks relaxed and comfortable, and I am incensed.

"How long do you plan to sit relaxing while I'm in the other room feeding the girls and trying to get them to sleep?!" I demand. The inclination to assume the worst in Jon, to assume I'm completely alone in this new enterprise, causes no end of rifts and trouble. Like most sleep-deprived new parents, Jon doesn't respond well to this worst-case scenario assumption mechanism and reacts in kind. Before we know it, we're embroiled in a war of who is working harder, who cares more, who cares less, who is a good parent, who is bad, uncaring, and selfish. The words and resentments fly.

He looks up and says, "I'm just taking a few minutes to myself. I need some time alone."

Stricken by the sure knowledge that this is the sound of our relationship ending, I slink back to the room with quiet tears of defeat. When he comes in a few minutes later, he is conciliatory and rests his hand on my knee.

"Listen, babe, don't take it personally that I need time to myself. I'm really just not that into babies, but I love you and I love our girls. Infants are just hard for me. I don't really like babies."

I try to remain calm as we speak, but adrenaline is shooting through my brain and alarm bells are sounding.

He doesn't like babies. He doesn't like babies.

I am grateful that it is dark and he can't see my terror-stricken face. I put on a brave voice and respond, "So you don't like infants, we can work with that. You don't have to do this with me, you know. I could do this alone if I had to. Don't feel obligated to stay if you don't want to."

Wisely recognizing this "offer" as a fake, he reassures again. "Hey. I want to stay. I love you. This is just a huge transition for me. That's all. I'm going to have a hard time with this."

Mommy Doesn't Drink Here Anymore

Nothing can take away the sting of his words. My only beloved, with whom I am one, doesn't like our babies. No matter what fairy tale of new babyhood I've adopted, this is the beginning of a grudge I hold against him. A small wedge that begins working its way between us, the in-love couple destined to be together always.

After three months, Jon calls me one day as excited and happy as I've heard him since the twins were born.

"Rachael! I found us the perfect place! It's close to downtown, bus lines, has two bedrooms, an office, and a laundry room. It's cozy and within our budget. Will you come take a look?"

We take the place immediately and make ready to move our three-month-old twins into our new home. I remember our first night there, proudly making chicken and setting our cozy little kitchen table for Jon and me. The twins sit in their swings while Mommy and Daddy eat and soak up the immense relief of having our own house again.

I remember unpacking the boxes and then collapsing them down outside, in between running inside to feed and play with the twins. At three months postpartum, I am feeling better but still heavier than I want to be and very weepy. I'm continually blown away by the sheer magnitude and exhaustion of new baby twins. I feel utterly unprepared, trying to keep afloat through sheer willpower. I am also completely underprepared for how utterly lonely new mother-hood is for me. I resent how dependent I am on Jon. I resent him his freedom from breastfeeding, and from the neurotic overconcern that plagues me at every turn.

I have never ever been this angry to be a woman. Angry to the core. I am unable to articulate or communicate to anyone how trapped I feel by this new biological life. I'm mushy and soft, and drippy and gooey, and everything clicks when I walk around. I used to be free to roam the woods, and rope swing over a huge gully, to run 3 miles a day, to go wherever I want whenever I want. To be free.

So I start to drink each evening, and it helps smooth out the rough edges. I count the hours until bedtime, and then I set up my wineglass next to a read-ing chair and exult in the few hours of freedom and relaxation afforded after each long, wearisome day.

By the time the twins are four months old, Jon and I are barely speaking, all vestiges of our passionate love completely obliterated by our current circumstances. I spend my evenings preparing for the twins' bed-time. I sing them songs and rock them to sleep, after which I reward myself with quiet hours reading in a comfortable blue chair with a few glasses of wine as an accompaniment. I mark this as the beginning of my devolution into problem drinking and then alcoholism.

I know now that this is postpartum depression. Jon's layoff, my highly responsible, exhausting, full-time job in public finance, and sleep deprivation erode whatever mental health I've mustered to date. Before long, I worry that I'm utterly failing as a mother and a partner. I'm completely disoriented and drowning. I can't even begin to ask for help because I already have so much help from my mom and stepmom, who both babysit the twins in those first months.

I worry and fret and toss and turn about all the things I might be doing wrong. And I drink.

It doesn't take long for these winds of Mother Guilt to take root in my soul. I just know that all the other (better) mothers are happily at home making cookies or cleaning things or disciplining children patiently, while the comforting smells of wholesome foods (organic) drift through the house (clean and owned outright), while their handsome, supportive husbands sit at the kitchen table talking about Truth or God or The Way Things Work. In this fabled Other Mother Realm, there is never brokenness or yelling or uncertainty or fear. These women never lean in tentatively and whisper, "My life feels completely empty." They live in a world I will never inhabit, so I don't even try. I am a failure at love.

As my previously lust- and laugh-filled relationship unravels under the multiplying pressures, Jon and I both stand by feeling absolutely helpless in the face of our familial deterioration. We do all the usual things—counseling, books, screaming matches, making up, sane discussions of our future, chore division lists—but nothing, nothing takes away the heartache. Not one thing.

Even with all the fighting and heartbreak, Jon still makes me salivate. Even now, with all his daughters and me, his puffy angry partner in tow, he is beautiful. I love to watch him move around the room, I love him in the dark, but I do not love his unwillingness to coparent in the way I expect.

Mostly, I can't believe I've been hoodwinked into this situation of total emotional dependence on a man. A man who can choose whether or not to stay in the room while I feed the babies, who retains his choice in the matter, while I feel tethered and torn up by the ordeal. Plundered and pillaged and left for dead, but also tenderized to the core, unable to conjure the body armor love has always required.

And I simply cannot get over it. I cannot forgive him for not loving me the way I need him to. In fairness, we are equally dumbstruck in the face of this brokenness.

I'm coming unglued. And even though I'm thirty-three, I have very few close women friends who have kids, so I feel alone and untethered. I go to one of those "Mommy and Me" support groups, but I'm much too afraid and proud to sully the happy get-together with the truth: I have no idea how to do this. I look around and think everyone else is happily married and delighted by motherhood. I'm alone like I've never ever been alone in my entire life. I want my partner to save me, and he simply can't. I'm drowning.

I later learn that having babies, especially mul-
tiples, is a great predictor of marital unhappiness
and divorce. Our not being married and together
only a year when the twins are born makes matters
worse. Statistically, our misery is as predictable as the
child of an alcoholic becoming an alcoholic herself.
I hate statistics. It doesn't help that when I become
a mother, my biological imperative and heart's desire
to feed, clothe, and keep my babies safe, loved, and
warm leaves room for little else. I become a she-lion
with a den only big enough for my babies and me. So
when anyone else tries to come in, no matter how
beloved, even if they bring food and a much-needed
break, I can't let down my guard. Even my beloved is
suspect, even now when I need him more than ever.
The father of my babies is a stranger. And I simply
don't know how to cross back over and take his hand.
We're completely stuck.

So I leave.

CHAPTER 3

single mama, dry with a twist

I pack up my baby twins and leave. I don't know how I think I can do this, but I tell myself it's for the best. In retrospect I see that depression and sadness and despair drove me away, more than reason or circumspect decision making. At the time, I'm simply unable to make a reasonable decision. I am totally heartbroken and exhausted.

He cries and asks me to stay. His heart is broken, but I don't see that. I refuse to live this way. If I'm going to effectively be a single parent, I might as well be one through and through. I am a failure at love.

I buy a small house more than an hour north of my job, then flex my hours so that by leaving the house at 5 A.M. I can be home by 3 P.M. each day and have the afternoon with the twins. My mother, God love her very soul, comes down to watch my babies while I work, asking nothing in return. The other two days, I work from home. The twins' dad has them each Friday night and Saturday. And when they're at their father's house, I drink with abandon.

The twins are sick a lot this first year, and I miss tons of work. We all get pneumonia, then stomach flu, then colds. They sleep poorly at night and so do I. I only sleep the whole night through when they're with their father. The rest of the time I'm queen mother of the caribou herd, hunted stealthily and steadily by the arctic fox that I do not see but can sense and smell. He's going to attack, and I must hold vigil over my most beloved. I'm exhausted and crazy. I'm in Crazy Mommy World.

Mommy Doesn't Drink Here Anymore

When I get home from work, my mom and the girls are usually playing quietly in the living room while the late afternoon sun pours in through the huge, single-paned, pretty windows. This place is freezing in the winter; I turn the heat up very high and not one person complains. It is my house. These are my bills. This is our very own cozy cottage. I love this house. It is trim and tidy and small, with a huge flat yard and a small strip of narrow concrete out front that looks like an unfinished walkway. We call it "the runway," and the twins are biplanes circling around, landing, and then taking off again. They wobble and toddle around the yard, their tiny baby legs so short, it must seem like miles. We're all fenced in here, and though life is hard, this home I have with my babies slowly feels safer and more secure as time goes on. It helps that no one is near enough to break my heart.

The twins and I go on walks in the afternoons, and I like to stop into the store down the road to buy a bottle of wine every week or so, then every few days, then every evening. I put them to bed, fingers crossed, every night hoping they'll sleep through, though they rarely do. Of course, I have more support than many people: parents who babysit, an employer that allows flextime and telecommuting, a house of my own, two healthy daughters, and an ex who pays child support on time and never misses a visit. But even with all of the logistical support, I still feel broken.

I often wonder if it would have been easier had I stayed with the twins' father. It's all speculation, projection, and rewriting history now. He has long since happily married, and when I see him and his wife together, I realize that we never could have been happy like that, not in that peaceful way, not in that everything-is-going-to-be-just-fine kind of way. He and I still spark and fight and argue. She fits him to a T, while I never did. After surviving each other, we both need a safe haven. And both of us, in our own way, find exactly what we were looking for.

Nine months after the twins' dad and I split, I'm ready to start dating again. I start using online dating services and strike up an email relationship with a man one town over who has never been married and who is three years my junior. When I broach the subject of my children (Does he want any?), he seems open to my kids, though we both agree meeting them isn't a good idea until we know each other better. He and I go on a few dates and chat about books and our lives.

He seems miraculously baggage free, handsome, and shy. He is domestic, likes to cook and clean, and keeps his home and garden in good order. He seems safe and kind and interested in me. We get along just fine.

Like me, he is a Seattle transplant who telecommutes to work. He and I spend several months getting to know each other, and he slowly gets to know the twins. Our first days together as a family are spent during a laid-back, sunny, cool summer. I've cashed out my retirement to take a few months off from my high-stress job, so for the first time since the twins' birth I have no work to get to or schedule to keep. He's able to spend hours in the afternoons with us, and he and I drink together and enjoy the lazy days. I can't remember how much we drink, only that it is part of our shared landscape, our peaceful, quiet, happy landscape. We are technically dating, but in reality he spends every night at our house, and soon our future seems inevitable.

I host a brunch at my house for my Seattle friends to meet him. He stays in the kitchen to cook for everyone, and they, predictably, approve. How different he is from Jon! Humble, approachable, interested in young children, babies even! What a miracle to have found someone like him in less than a year after breaking up with the twins' dad. It is a seemingly simple and very happy ending. My family meets and loves him. My two brothers take him to lunch and ask his intentions (this time, they're not messing around). Maybe I've finally lucked out. Maybe this is just as it appears. Good timing, great luck, a wonderful and easy forever-after predicted by all. Nothing but blue skies as far as the eye can see.

After six months we get engaged while on a weekend getaway in Vancouver, British Columbia.

We are wrestling around on the bed and he is holding my arms and laughing. . . .

"Hey Rachael."

"Yesssss?"

"Would you marry me?"

"I'd love to!"

Even then, the idea of getting engaged after only
six months seems a bit fast, but I justify it by saying we've gotten to know each other more quickly
because of the babies. He's there at 2 A.M. when I
give the twins their bottles. He's helped diaper, rock,
and feed them. He's helped them swim in their little
turtle wading pool. But in another way, I am oddly
passive about this decision. He is part of our daily
life, involved in the nooks and crannies of childrearing. He shows great promise as a father and husband.
And I'm so determined that I rush headlong into our
next phase . . . the paint barely dry on our first date.

We celebrate our engagement with a bottle of
Wild Goose Viognier from a British Columbian
winery. I gulp down several glasses until I am
warmly glowing. Here I sit—newly engaged and
newly tipsy.

This time I'm going to get it right. I'm going to be
kind, loving, and patient. I'm going to make this marriage happy and give my daughters the security they
deserve. Finally.

My daughters.

They are two and a half on the day we marry, and
they're wearing pretty bluebell dresses with capes
and flowery hair clips. My dress is black with steel
blue glass beads, black boots, and a dyed navy blue
veil. The dress feels fantastic! I stand under the trellis

waiting for the photographer to snap some pictures. I feel like myself.

I'd had another white dress picked out until three days prior to the wedding. It was traditional with matching shoes. My mom and stepmom had come with me, as had my lovely twelve-year-old niece. But when I try it on a few days before the wedding, it feels all wrong. Something is terribly wrong. I think it's the dress.

I call my mom, who is gangbusters ready to find me another dress. We look around and I see it. The evening gown-cum-second-wedding dress, and I know it's perfect for the occasion. Nontraditional, with a hint of darkness and rebellion, still a wedding dress, my wedding dress. I am hopeful that I can figure out how to be the sort of wife signified by this dress: loving and kind, but with a flair for drama and a touch of darkness besides.

Our wedding day is a grand sunny wintry day, and the wedding is on a homey little farm near where Jack and I live. The twins spend most of the Solstice Day ceremony crying, "Mama! Mama!" Mommy is standing in the front of the room without them. Eventually grandma quiets them with crackers and escorts them next door to the barn where we'll have dinner.

The day the twins and I get ready to move into Jack's house I can't stop crying. His mom is very sweet and understanding and keeps saying things like "Change is hard." But that isn't it. I hide in Jack's bathroom and call my mom sobbing.

"Why am I so sad? Shouldn't I be happy?"

"Oh honey, I don't know. Did something happen? Did you and Jack get into a fight?" she asks.

"No. It's not that. I'm just sad that I'm leaving my little house."

I hide in the bathroom talking to her for a while longer, and then I try and put myself back together enough to reappear. My brothers are moving my furniture and are talking with Jack and slapping him on the back as they come in and out of the house. They're all getting quite friendly. My brothers trust and like Jack. They figure he's making an honest woman out of me. Or at least that's what I think they're thinking.

It doesn't even occur to me that perhaps we should stay in our very own little house. His house is bigger. And this time, I'm doing the practical thing come hell or high water. Life, for a while, is grand. It's very lovely, once we get settled, to have someone who enjoys cooking and helps so much with the girls. I take most of the responsibility, but his regular daily help is so much greater than any the twins' dad ever offered. I am more grateful and relieved every day.

At the same time, he frequently loses his temper with the twins and has higher expectations of them than I do, but these differences are natural. He has a huge adjustment and being a stepparent is a thankless and wearisome job. I talk to him about it and ask him to let me take charge of discipline. He insists that if we're going to be a family, he needs to be allowed to weigh in on childrearing. I reluctantly agree. There are several times that I intervene when I feel he's too rough, or scary, or loud. We're all incredibly anxious, and no one is sleeping well.

He changes jobs and has a few months home with us, so I hope that our time as a family will solidify our bonds and smooth out the rough edges. He and I usually have a drink in the evening, but it's nothing too much and no one gets drunk. I do miss romance, and I notice that we very quickly fall into patterns it seems like other married couples take years to achieve—some of them good, some of them more like treating each other like furniture. Our sex life is fraught; our childrearing differences are difficult to negotiate; we have diverging philosophies about money and in-laws. In under a year, we are poster children for what can go wrong with second marriages, but we are in this for good. And we stick things out.

Saying blended families aren't easy is like saying it hurts when you run over your foot with a sport utility vehicle, but even knowing this, the transition for my husband from bachelor to husband and stepfather and my transition from single mother to wife and shared parent is a rocky one. I learn later that the drinking only makes this situation worse, less tenable. I have only a bleary checked-out mind to walk through what should have been a hardworking, counseling-filled conscious effort to make our blended family work. But it isn't all dreary struggling. After a year, I am pregnant with another little girl. The pregnancy and birth bring us very close together for a while. He and I both adore her. Our family is so lovely now . . . but the underlying fissures in our relationship are only widened by my quickly resumed drinking.

It's been all childrearing and kitchen cleaning and new babies since we met. Two years after marrying, we get pregnant with our very own little baby. She is the undisputed apple dumpling of his eye and mine. A jewel. But also one more person, one more thing between us, to keep us focused on everything but just him and me.

Rather than pay attention to what is happening, I have more to drink.

plastered

I nod and aim a fake smile at the group of parents streaming into the kindergarten classroom. I sit in an impossibly small wobbly chair and pray for the familiar combination of nausea, self-loathing, and light-headedness to subside. As the teacher welcomes us and begins walking through a typical day, I lean in to hear more and immediately jump up and run out of the room in search of a restroom, a bucket, or a garbage can.

I stop to consider that drinking that bottle and a half of wine the night prior, despite plans to have much less, might not have been very wise. Here I am the next day paying the piper, like someone in a B movie, playing the role of Irresponsible Mother, sitting on the hard floor of what looks like the Seven Dwarfs' bathroom, shaking and heaving, praying no one walks in. I sit unmoving, resting my head on my arms for nearly an hour. I end up missing the whole open house, and for the first time I begin to wonder if I'm an alcoholic.

Since becoming a mother five years before, I've longed to hang on to a part of myself that isn't smeared in Mommy goo. The part that laughs at parties, looks good in heels, and earns a living while spending quality time with loved ones. I want to be the anti-June Cleaver, the un-wife, the un-mother, loving and present, but not invisible or brainless. And while it is gravely oversimplifying to say this is why I drink, drinking does begin as a bulwark against the onslaught of mama drones, an enjoyable evening ritual, a life raft—cheaper and easier to do with young children than yoga or running. Only later does it become the best part of every day.

As my marriage starts having more bad days than good, I feel like a thirty-six-year-old woman with a true gift for picking the wrong men. When you are raising young children, it is utterly frightening how quickly your relationship can devolve; how swiftly you stop talking about anything but dinners and laundry and school outings and grocery shopping. If there are dark ominous clouds hanging over our house, I don't see them clearly. All I know is that I'm exhausted and lonely and can barely see straight. And of course, I'm drinking more now than ever. I begin to wonder if I'm ever going to be able to provide a stable, happy life for my daughters.

The thing about parenting in this situation is that the walls between you and marital happiness seem inexplicably high and insurmountable. So I come to a decision: Regardless of my unhappiness, I'll soldier away so that my kids might have the stability and consistency they deserve. I decide that throwing my shoulder to the wheel on this one is the right thing to do. No wonder I'm so tired all the time. At some point along the way, I make a few deals with the devil. *If you let me be in love with someone else, I'll stay. If I can keep drinking, I'll stay.* Martyrdom doesn't suit me very well.

These deals I make with the universe under cover of darkness are deadly, particularly when they try to guarantee happiness for my children. As if the universe is a vending machine, where happy endings can be purchased if one has correct change; a matter of odds and probabilities rather than luck, chance, healthy living, and hard work. As if I can bargain for my children's lives.

Are other mothers like me? Do they believe they should lay down their lives for their children, if not literally, then figuratively? Since I'm not in sub-Saharan Africa, or Iraq, or on the brink of homelessness or poverty, I prove my love and devotion by setting aside my own happiness for theirs.

I'm hopeful to undo the last generation's erroneous belief that happy marriages mean happy children, and that two people locked in marital warfare are better off free, and so are the kids. In my experience growing up, no-fault divorce made way for no-fault desperately grieving children. In sixth grade, after my parents divorced, I remember standing on that playground with an empty pit in my stomach, thinking I was the only kid whose parents didn't live together anymore. Wondering whose house I would choose. As if anyone could choose to live without a heart, a liver, a lung. As if anyone could pick whether to amputate their right or their left leg.

Even with these memories, I understand what a relief it must have been—after generations of unspoken misery, of housewifely serfdom, to break free of social judgment and constraints; to take a lover, or a job; to live independently for the first time since marrying in one's early twenties. I can and do understand, but I also know what it is like to be a child whose parents divorce. I know what it is like to have one's world ripped into pieces.

And so I bargain away and hope for the best and pray that some clarity or answer will fall from the sky, all the while living with someone who is a stranger to my heart, but whom I care for and respect and see as a friend, someone who helps raise my daughters as his own, not perfectly, but with hearty effort and consistent presence. That we have little chemistry or deep connection seems irrelevant to the mother in me. Besides, I say to myself, no one raising young children has time for anything but stories, cooking, cleaning, and baths anyway. It may feel empty and frightening and hopeless, but at least our family is intact.

Drinking gives me bargaining power and helps me keep my commitments. I've never been married this long, never been able to stick it out, but on another level this is sick. And this level of illness seeps so deeply into my bones that by the time I try to get sober, I feel like I need a whole new skeletal structure, a new heart, and a brand new mind.

On the surface I stay sassy and edgy and champion other mothers' need for time alone, for love and reading, for many worlds beyond raising young children. In public I am the rebellious swearing mama who is lively, saucy, and driven. In private, I shudder in fear in the corner, as I lie myself into believing that alcohol isn't the destination, only a ticket to the real journey.

I can force this marriage to work. I can control my drinking. I can cajole my husband to be who I need him to be.

I want to be the kind of mother who never talks about diapers or potty training, who doesn't dream of boring you with which child did or didn't wake Mommy up last night. I want to be the kind of mother who loves her children without losing herself and whose sassy sense of humor is slightly off kilter, and makes husbands deeply uncomfortable. "I need this," I say to myself while pouring that first glass of a crisp white into a pretty glass. My shoulders relaxing, I look at my three kids through narrowing warrior eyes and think, "Bring it!"

But wine as proxy for happiness and joy, as something mind expanding and extraordinary, doesn't work very well in the long run. At least it doesn't for me, and very quickly a few glasses becomes nearly a bottle and then more; all day thinking, *When can I drink?!*

I like to believe that alcohol vaults me beyond my limitations as a child-corralling frump, a working stiff with a second shift in the evenings, but all it really ever does is wipe me out and shut me down to the pain of living in the world when one refuses to admit the truth. It's not clear how long this downward spiral takes, or when I begin shaking in the mornings, or dialing a helpline and hanging up, or when I start lying to myself about my own unhappiness.

Other than to my children and a few close women friends, I rarely tell the full truth to other people in my life, revealing instead only small parts of the story, as they enhance or add amusement to whatever circumstances require: sassy mama friend, responsible employee, faithful wife, adoring mother.

There is a real life hidden in there somewhere, but it is buried underneath denial and a whole bellyful of liquor. I'm the puppet, and alcohol is the puppet master. This inclination to hold some things back, stay quiet and private, is of course intrinsic to the human condition (especially when one has children, a mortgage, and a marriage). The trouble begins when the faking and the leaving out gets bigger than the whole truth, until eventually the actor becomes the story that he has written for himself and the play isn't even true anymore. There is no possibility of real connection because everything is an animated cartoon and there is nothing to hold on to.

What began as a life philosophy, as a cool refreshing glass of wine on a sunny patio with friends, was turning into an addiction and a spiritual disease. It ceased being about relaxation and fun and slipped down into just getting by, barely surviving the motherhood thing, and the life thing. It began to require an ever-increasing amount of liquid support.

I start doubting my ability to get by, a doubt that wears away my confidence and turns me into a person living on wishes and dreams and hopes for a better day, that will always, inevitably, happen later. Later—the curse of those, like me, under the misapprehension that life is an endless boundary water to be dribbled and drabbled away while the real story, in which I emerge triumphant and in a ball gown, is delayed again and again. For those like me, who rely on the fiction of a perfect tomorrow, drinking is an absolutely fabulous pastime—just enough of something to keep real life at bay.

As the un-June Cleaver, I mock the notion that as the mother I am the emotional center of my home. I resent my own importance and so try to shrink down, and simply refuse to matter as much as I really do, but motherhood hunts me down and feeds on me like a cat feeds on a broken-winged bird. It is not optional, and not fungible. It cannot be gotten rid of, at least it can't for me.

Somehow I've lost the belief that I can handle motherhood and marriage. How can I, who am so obviously flawed, have these beautiful and blameless small people in my charge? Motherhood gets too big to manage, and I want to be perfect. I want to be everything good and loving and patient and kind. I want to save my daughters from every sick, broken part of the human heart, especially if that sickness and brokenness belongs to their mother. I only realize much later that the drinking makes everything worse. Much worse.

One afternoon, I start drinking at 1 P.M. This early afternoon drinking is starting to seem like a very good idea, and it happens with greater regularity. When I take that first sip, I feel decadent and rebellious. My stomach is warm and ticklish and my spirits immediately lift. I look like a 10-cent sommelier breathing in the sweet white wine, dreaming of all the good things that will happen later. This afternoon, the kids are playing outside, and I sit on the back porch and watch them perform their headstands and kicks and floats with calls of "Look Mama!" and "Watch this!" echoing in my ears. I'm slowly fading away from them, but they don't seem to mind or notice as long as I nod and agree that this or that trick is fabulous. My older daughter later acknowledges that sometimes I use a "pretend" voice, and I figure this sunny fake afternoon voice is the one to which she is referring. I'm so checked out that I don't notice until several seconds later that my youngest is struggling in the pool. My little golden-haired angel.

I throw down the glass and leap up to grab her out. She's sputtering and scared, but fine. I'm not. I'm gripped by the sure knowledge that any number of terrible catastrophes could befall my kids if I drink like this. I'm completely flattened, floored, and humbled. I pledge right that moment to lay off. When my husband comes home that evening, I tell him that I want to "cut back" my drinking, but without telling him of the afternoon's catastrophe. He heartily agrees that this is a good idea and asks what he can do to help. "Nothing. I can do it," I say, and I decide that what I need to do is try much harder.

For two days I don't drink anything, but I'm shaky and worried and impatient. Pretty soon, I decide that a glass or two is fine as long as it's after

5 P.M. And so for many months, I decide that my kids will be safe as long as I drink after my husband gets home from work. And if I can keep from drinking heavily until after their relatively early bedtime, they won't be any worse for it.

I fall asleep regularly very early, and I pick fights with my husband. I'd been so ignorant of the signs of alcoholism, despite growing up with a practicing alcoholic, that I didn't realize all this falling asleep early was really passing out.

In my quest to avoid wearing an apron and losing my brain, I harbor a deadly desire to be everything to my daughters, and therefore, eventually, nothing to myself. Throw in a beef casserole, and I am actually worse than June Cleaver. I am the neurotic stepsister of Snow White, Cinderella, and all the girls sleeping forever and waiting for the prince's kiss. Fast asleep until I can bear my own imperfection, the road winds downward, until I stop.

One night, I am drinking when I look up after spraying some words around and see where they have landed. Like shrapnel, they have torn through the tenderness of our late evening family room, where the children have so recently unloaded the toy box and spilled graham crackers on the floor. Though they are now upstairs asleep, we can still hear their echoes, and it is just the two of us remaining. I in my stupor, and he in his chair.

I remember saying something akin to "I don't love you anymore. How can you bear to stay with me knowing how I feel?"

Mommy Doesn't Drink Here Anymore

I can't remember the exact words, only the after-effects: the look of someone involved in an emotional prizefight left standing in the ring, surprised that someone so small and previously kind can deliver such a deft right hook. Surprised and hurt and quiet.

He says this to me: "Rachael, you're becoming mean."

And I stop and listen to the sound of my own undoing.

PART TWO

toward
recovery

first 30 days: alcohol is the love of my life

I have never been this lonely in my life. I feel like a finger puppet with no finger, ill and wrecked and many decades older than thirty-nine. I keep checking the mirror to see if some voodoo has happened that renders my insides visible from the outside. Of course if that were the case, I'd look like one of those shriveled apple dolls and no one would want to sit by me on the couch, so I take extra care with my makeup and shoes, warding off the inevitable discovery of my true colors by all those within my poisonous proximity.

I'm nauseous and shaky, and it is slowly dawning on me that whatever this muddle is, I need some help. It's not like one morning I tire of the hangovers and the lies and say, "Well. Looks like it's time for you to get help, Old Gal." It's more a creeping feeling that starts to take residence in my gut. I need someone to put a quilt around my shoulders and hold me for a week. But I'm the mother. An adult. Likely no one is going to do that anytime soon. Certainly not my husband, who is so pissed and hurt he can barely look at me. I've wrecked what we had by being so lost and scared and mean.

And unfaithful.

After a few years of marriage, I'd gotten involved with a man who lived about 60 miles away. We met through work, and it didn't take long for my loneliness to justify seeking solace somewhere other than my marriage; never mind that each time my lover and I met, we drank copious amounts of alcohol, drowning our respective marital complaints in a sea of wine and whiskey. I wasn't sorry at all. I wasn't angry. I wasn't guilty. I was taking care of myself (since my husband wouldn't) and finding the love and passion I deserved (which he wasn't capable of giving me).

It seems unpardonable now, but then, it seemed just fine.

In my 12-Step group people talk about how our addictions damage our moral compass. I suppose that might seem a tad convenient. If one can simply excuse all bad behavior with a breezy, "Oh that? That's just my addiction," it would be ridiculous and absolutely unfair. Luckily, true amends go significantly deeper than that. Each person has to review her own behaviors (once her brain has cleared) and decide how, where, and in which matters she owes amends.

My amends and the full realization of the damage I'd caused were many months away on the afternoon I decide to pick up the phone and call the 800-number in the phonebook.

I dial the 12-Step helpline a few times but chicken out and hang up. I imagine the conversation: "Oh hi there. I'm not sure if I'm an alcoholic but I could really use someone to come over here and snuggle with me for a week. Do you have anyone who could do that? Or just read to me from *Anne of Green Gables* or something, while feeding me Rocky Road ice cream?"

Instead, what I say is this: "Oh hi. I must have dialed the wrong number. Thanks, byeeeeee." Click.

I'm sure that never happens to them.

Still, the vague premonition of doom eventually impels me to take notice of the objective facts of my life. Like a detached accountant, I review my life thus far: I am inexplicably unhappy and lonely. I don't stay in jobs for long. I move every two years. Despite changing everything around with great regularity, there is a hole in my heart. I keep trying to fill it with children and work and lovers, but nothing really works for long. I know something is very wrong here. And I think my drinking might be making it worse. For once I start from the inside rather than the outside, and I know that my drinking is a good place to begin.

I know this like the person going over a waterfall in the barrel knows landing on the rocks below will hurt like hell. It is the whispering voice in the back of my head each night as I lift the glass to my lips:

I can't stop.

I need to stop.

Why can't I stop?

Finally I turn to someone I've always been able to talk to without fear of judgment or recrimination or insistence that I hang my head in shame: my younger brother Jim. When we were kids, I used to call him "Our Little Man of Joy," and the name still fits. He's funny and humble and incredibly loving. If we weren't siblings, we'd be very good friends. I dial his cell phone, and all of a sudden I feel embarrassed.

My heart is pounding. I pull over to the side of the road in front of a jewelry store with several huge posters of happy (thin, nondrinking, perfect) women covered in diamonds from adoring husbands. The caption reads, "Show her you still care."

If I were in this poster, it would say, "Sure she drinks too much and is unfaithful, but isn't she grand?"

Unfortunately, my brother picks up after just two rings.

"Hey Jimmy, it's me. I want to talk to you about something. Do you have a minute?"

"Hey Rach, how are you? I've got plenty of time to talk. I'm on my way home from work. What's up?"

I start laughing. "Oh, it's really nothing. Nothing serious."

The twins are starting school in two weeks. Maybe I'll wait until then to bring this up.

"Rachael?"

"So here's the thing. I'm pretty sure I don't drink as much as Mom used to, but sometimes I wonder if I might be drinking too much."

Quiet on the other end of the line.

Jim's serious voice: "How much do you drink?"

"How much?" I laugh.

Oh, a gallon a day.

"A few glasses of wine each evening. Sometimes more."

"How much more?" he asks. Deep, fatherly type voice.

"Three glasses?" I answer tentatively, hoping he won't sense how much I'm lying.

More like six. Okay, ten.

"Is your drinking a problem?" he persists.

"No. I haven't gotten into trouble. No one tells me I drink too much. I haven't gotten a DUI if that's what you mean."

"Rachael, if you think you have a problem, you probably do. Have you called a 12-Step program?"

"Jimmy, the thing is I haven't really decided whether I need to stop yet. I was hoping you could help me figure out what to do." I tell him this, but I'm hoping he'll reassure me that I'm overreacting.

Instead, he says, "Well, if you called me because you're worried, then what's keeping you from just stopping?"

Because giving up alcohol forever is about the most depressing thought imaginable.

"I probably will stop, Jim; I just don't really want to stop right now."

"Okay then. When are you going to stop?"

"Maybe tomorrow," I reassure him, switching into my mature, career-woman voice. "I think tomorrow would be good. I have a few more weeks until the girls start school, so maybe I'll stop once the stress of that transition is over."

"Rach. Why not stop today?"

"Well. I don't know. I guess maybe because I don't want to? I'm not ready to give it up? Listen, just forget I said anything. Please don't say anything to Dad or Mom. Please don't talk about this with anyone."

Silence on the other end. And then, "Will you please just stop today? I don't know that much about addiction and recovery, but I understand once you make up your mind to quit, it can get pretty ugly pretty fast."

"Great. Just great. Something to look forward to, I guess. Okay, Jimmy, I guess I'll stop today." I say it out loud, and then my stomach starts to ache and I'm afraid.

How will I give it up? How will I get by?

"Can you get to a 12-Step meeting? I'm going to call you later tonight to check and see if you've stopped."

"What? You're checking up on me now?" Jim and I joke around all the time, but we've never had to check up on each other before and I'm not sure I like it. I took on more of a motherly role with him when we were younger, but it's clear that now the tables have turned.

"Yes, Rachael, I am going to check up on you."

"Well then. I guess I better make some calls. And Jim? I love you too."

And the call ends. I sit in the car as the full extent of the situation sinks in. I've just admitted to someone else that I have a drinking problem.

Fabulous. Younger brother as ninja interventionist. I need to keep my word to him, otherwise he'll keep bugging me about this.

Later that afternoon, I drive to a local park and pull the car over to sit and contemplate the call I need to make. The people in the park appear cheery and non-hung over. My hands are shaking as I dial the

800-number, this time with the intention of actually saying something.

A woman picks up the phone sounding very, very friendly and helpful. I ask if there is a meeting anywhere nearby, and she tells me there is one starting in 5 minutes only 2 miles from here. The 12-Step meetings in my town are organized not only by topic (literature study, open discussion) and status (open only to alcoholics, open to anyone) but also by gender (women-only and men-only meetings as well as those open to all). For people like me, this menu system helps eliminate another excuse for not going.

✳ ✳ ✳

The small squat building sits in the middle of a manufacturing plant parking lot and looks like a cross between a shack and a bomb shelter. I walk in and take a seat at the back. I'm still shaking as it dawns on me that this could be the beginning of the rest of my life, which does not fill me with joy. My first impression is not favorable. The carpet is gray and stained, and the room smells like stale cigarettes (of course). There is a leader up front, and she asks if anyone is here for their first meeting. A woman sitting directly in front of me raises her hand and introduces herself. She has long red hair, and after saying her name, she starts to cry. I raise my hand.

Are you supposed to raise your hand?
"Hi. I'm Rachael, and I'm an alcoholic."

The woman at the front welcomes us. "Wow. We love first-timers here! Welcome! We're so glad you're here!" and I immediately think of the Mormon Church.

When I started attending the Mormon Church in high school, everyone was so welcoming and friendly and seemed so sincere. I was this lonely fourteen-year-old band girl barely 5 feet tall with glasses, and when the nice Mormon ladies would make me lunch or invite me to dinner, I'd be so grateful to be included and cared for. I'd sit and compliment their casseroles and corn and smile and try to be helpful so they'd let me stay a little longer. Their preteen kids would complain about all the rules and the boredom, and I'd sit in their rec rooms and say, "Yeah. I know. How annoying," but secretly I'd smile and love every minute of it.

The people in this meeting seem just like those Mormon ladies. No doubt all the friendliness in the room makes some people suspicious, but maybe I'm just broken enough not to care if they are faking. This meeting is still the nicest place I've been in a long time. I wonder if they'd let me live here. I wonder if they let people bring their kids. I close my eyes and will time to stand still.

I feel someone put her arm around my shoulders and tell me everything will be okay, and I realize I'm crying. Apparently, people here are especially kind to broken people. Maybe I should raise my hand and admit some other things too. "I had an affair. I had children out of wedlock. I look all put together but I'm broken. I need someone to save me." Instead, I sit and breathe and listen to the other ladies talk about how much they loved to drink, how this program helped them get happy. The chairperson laughs about how hung over she used to be each morning, how much she loves men, and how many failed marriages she has. I really like that in a woman. She laughs, and the others laugh with her.

I look around and realize that I haven't felt this at home in years.

Soon the meeting ends and I'm given a list of phone numbers and a meeting schedule, and I decide to check out another meeting across town. I'm on automatic pilot. I keep saying over and over to myself, "I'm checking this out. It can't hurt to check it out. Just stop thinking and go to another meeting. This could work."

This could work.

And so it begins.

It.

My effort to get sober. To join up and check out the weird, happy people of this 12-Step program and see what medications they're on. I need whatever magic pills they're taking. Because these people laugh more than anyone I've met in my entire life other than my little brother Jim.

What I learn later is that alcoholism is a progressive disease, and I've only just begun to sense the outside edge of this beckoning darkness. I've recently touched the robes of the Dark King Alcohol, and rather than heal me, he's leading me straight to Hell.

I tell myself I'm checking this thing out, trying to decide if I'm an alcoholic or simply a problem drinker. I hope that I'll find the perfect 12-Step meeting and it will clarify whether I should stay or go. After a while, I decide I might not know any of these things for a long time.

My inner compass/decision machinery is all gummed up. The well part of me, the strong, loving part, seems to have completely disappeared. And in her place is someone who drinks every day, lies to her husband, and tries to figure out what went wrong. This life, that on the outside looks reasonably good, is an absolute wreck, unmanageable in the extreme.

I attend my second meeting in an even grimier building in an even more remote location, and I start doubting that this is where I belong. After all, I haven't had a DUI, or lost a job, or wrecked my car, or gotten hurt. My kids barely notice how much I drink, and I drink only at night (except in the summer or on sunny days or when the day is especially rough). Nevertheless, something from these meetings is touching me, something about people telling the truth and being honest. Even if I'm not an alcoholic, this place feels good and I can probably learn something here. There is a very small opening in my mind that allows me to think that this might make my life better. Quitting drinking is another matter altogether.

As soon as I say out loud that I'm going to stop drinking for a while, white wine is all I can think about. I become obsessed with what I'm not doing. Even if I successfully lay off for a few days, I can't shake the image of the glasses I'm not drinking. I can taste, smell, and conjure them from clouds or soda cans, or from my children's faces. Wine is everywhere and seemingly all-powerful. It is all I can do to stop myself from rushing to the store to buy gallons and gallons of wine to swim in, to live in.

I shake my head to clear out the thoughts, but they stay around, like a brain stain. Going to meetings helps for about 30 seconds, but alcohol has me by the gullet. Why can't I shake this thing? How can other people stop at just one or two, or even more puzzlingly, leave half a glass unfinished, while I guzzle as if I am storing up for a fraternity party that ended twenty years ago?

In addition to this fixation, there is the small matter of how much I need alcohol to do my life. To be a loving mother, hardworking employee, reasonable wife, I need alcohol. Or so I believe. I live at the intersection of postmodern Supermom and gypsy spirit. Freedom and liveliness and passion are more easily crammed into my busy schedule if I have a few drinks. Hell, the drinks *are* my liveliness and passion, my proxy for living a life that is more than cleaning floors, cooking grilled cheese sandwiches, and not being in love with my husband. I'm Alice in Wonderland with three small children, tight jeans, and a huge mortgage. I can shrink down, or rise up, with a few drinks or a magic pill. For me and other mothers like me, the Supermom fantasy has morphed from bringing home the bacon and frying it up in a pan into something far more dangerous, destructive, and dark: successful career, soul mate marriage, well-adjusted children who also incidentally speak a second language and are advanced in math and science. Who wouldn't drink with this kind of pressure? Who wouldn't want to die?

In the face of this, the meetings seem like a small peashooter against an army of wine-filled superpowered sniper rifles. I'm lost on my way to Dr. Seuss's perfect land, *Solla Sollew,* and I am one of the billions of birds all going the wrong way. Even when I find a meeting where I feel comfortable, where the people are friendly, warm, and accepting, and I manage not to drink for 17 days, it's hard as hell and I'm raw. I mark each day on my calendar, like I used to mark in the advancing days of each pregnancy, only instead of ultrasounds and doctor's appointments, I mark meeting times and locations.

Quitting drinking is very much like a bad breakup with The One Who Got Away. I see wine everywhere, dream of it, worry about when I'll see it next, eat too much candy, and am sure we will eventually work it out. I go from fiction and fantasy to nonfiction and recovery in a month, and the transition hurts my hair. As very quickly the face of things starts to melt away, revealing the shady, imperfect undersides of my very messy life, I cling to my good-on-paper list: the pretty children, the second husband, the good job, the nice house. All of this helps me feel better than most of the poor sots I sit next to in meetings. This inclination, to either feel better than or lower than dog dirt on a spoon, may be sympathetic and even charming in other people, but in oneself it's laughably grotesque. It is also incredibly human. And while the concept of not drinking a day at a time is intended to be comforting, all I can think is, *How?* Like someone who hasn't eaten a meal in three weeks watching someone cook dinner, I stare at the clock while Time, that bastard, obliges by slowing and dragging around so that I can hear the spider legs crawling along the floor. The meetings are usually only an hour long, but I shake my leg and shift in my chair and cannot get comfortable.

One evening I take all three girls to an old building that looks like a railway station. There is the telltale group of smokers out front, as well as the usual rundown *hoi polloi*. The room is long and narrow, with quotes like "Live and Let Live" and "Let Go and Let God" in cracked frames all hanging crookedly on dirty white backgrounds. Along one wall is an old church pew covered in well-used chair pads underneath a chalkboard listing birthdays and some kind of chore assignments. It smells of cedar and burned coffee, and the floor sags toward a huge bank of windows with a beautiful view of the bay. It reminds me of some of the Eagles' lodges they have in Seattle's older neighborhoods, places I used to go contra dancing, back in my square days. They've strung some small white lights, which makes the place feel safer and cozier than other meetings I've attended.

The girls play in the back section of the room with plastic dinosaurs and an old box of baby dolls. The fact that they let me bring my kids and have a makeshift but serviceable play area is a kindness parents of young children don't often encounter in new, non-kid-centered situations. At least I haven't. After all, I'm not at Gymboree or McDonald's Playland. And as we cross the room, negotiating snacks and squabbles, the people smile at us beneficently, and I feel less worried about the girls' noise and ruckus than I usually do in a public place. This warm, supportive reception also validates what I already know from my own experience: Alcoholism is a family disease. It makes sense they allow people to bring kids to meetings. I'm so grateful I start to cry.

A civilized glass of crisp white wine on a sunny patio would be delightful.

The thought, unwelcome and insistent, comes into my brain mere minutes after leaving the meeting. And so the argument begins, but on this day, I am weaker, more inclined to listen. As I load the girls into the car, I start thinking about drinking. It's a fine evening, and wouldn't it be relaxing to have a nice glass of wine with dinner? I never have just one, of course, but I tell myself that this time it's different. I've been sober 17 days and have learned a lot about drinking. This time I'll only have one. As the plan hatches, I set the wheels in motion. I tell the girls excitedly that we're going to have a special treat. We're going out to dinner at the place that gives kids balloons! They are thrilled. I feel my shoulders relax as I realize this 17-day ordeal is nearly over. Only 5 minutes after crying with gratitude I'm on the phone to my husband telling him to meet us at the restaurant, and I'm driving quickly to arrive there before him.

I tell myself I still haven't decided whether I'll order wine, but it's a lie. Before the waiter can even seat us, I order a glass. If he notices my loud voice as I order, he ignores it. And as he brings me the glass on a tray, I feel as if I've reconnected with a long-lost lover. It's frosty and sweet and pretty (Why does it always have to look so pretty and inviting?), and as I reach to take a sip, I feel something change. I put the glass back down on the table, and sit and decide to watch it for a while. Even while staring lovingly at the drink, for the first time in years I stop and consider the consequences of touching it to my lips. This pause, though brief, is something dramatically new and different. It is something that is related to the meetings I've attended and the people I've met, and their stories keep running through my mind. They've all had the same love/hate crush on drinking, all looked lovingly into the depths of their drinks of choice. Many of them have tried time and time again to stop drinking, and some have succeeded. If

Mommy Doesn't Drink Here Anymore

they can do it, can't I? If I can't go without drinking for longer than 17 days, doesn't that indicate I have a problem? I try and block out these thoughts and take a sweet first sip of wine, feel it warmly slide down my throat and into my stomach, which is soothed and relaxed for the first time in weeks. I drink it down and then I know something. To the depths of my soul I know that I need to have more than this one. That I need to drink more and more and more and that one will never ever be enough. This switch happens immediately. I can hear it click into place. The devil is in me again, and I'm back in the throes of this thing I can't shake.

And so the next plan is hatched. I'll convince my husband to take all three girls home from the restaurant, and I'll stop by the grocery store and pick up some more wine, or "supplies," as I've come to call it. The plan works. He agrees to take them home, and I promise to follow in my car.

As I watch the kids pile into my husband's car, I realize with a thrill that I am now free to drink or run away or both. I could get onto I-5 and never look back. I could hide away somewhere, find a new job, a new identity, a better, happier life.

Except for my daughters. My children, whom I love with every breath, even through the haze of alcohol. Whom I pretend to find inconvenient, but who are so precious to me that I can't avert my eyes when we're in the room together. I acknowledge the troubles of parenting, the exhaustion and the travails.

Sometimes this helps me lighten the terrible burden of responsibility. If I complain about sleep deprivation and laundry, I can put some distance between me and my loves, turning them into cartoon characters in the comic strip of my life. I want so many things for them: happy lives, wonderful educations, safety and health, a happy family. And increasingly, as I drink away my loneliness and misery, I cajole the universe, "Please, please let my daughters not have this kind of life. Please give them something much better." At the junction of dreaming for my daughters' future and owning up to the misery of my own life, I realize something needs to change.

As I watch them get into his car, I look down the road to two possible futures: the road to more drinking, and the road to somewhere else, presumably somewhere healthier and with fewer hangovers. These thoughts, inserted between my lust for alcohol and my plan to drink more today, suspend my plan of action just long enough so that I can madly search my car for a phone number, any phone number, from that women's meeting I attended the first day.

I call Helen, a young woman with nine years of sobriety, introduce myself, and blurt out the bone-shaking truth: "I can't live without alcohol. I simply can't. Furthermore, I'm pretty sure I'm not a real alcoholic."

Helen is very kind. She says she understands. She remembers what it's like to think the sun rises and sets on a bottle. She tells me it doesn't have to be this way. Can she take me to a meeting?

I agree to go.

She meets me at my house and drives me to the meeting.

For the next week, I sit in the back of what will later become my home group, with my hat pulled down over my eyes. I feel as if I'm the only person who has ever been through this. As if what I've done is the worst thing in human history. I get a sponsor, and she asks me if I've had enough yet. I say I have no idea. . . but I hope so. I hope I have. I want to learn to be happy, and to get out of this messy wreck of a life. She asks me to go to 90 meetings in 90 days, and I promise her I will.

I'm still not sure if I'm an alcoholic, but I decide to suspend my disbelief long enough to consider another way of doing things, even though I feel awful physically, emotionally, and spiritually. This is withdrawal, I'm told. And it is another piece of evidence in the mounting case against my drinking. I have always believed that I could stop anytime and began many days with a decision to take the night off from drinking. On the rare occasions when I do without, it is only with terrible twitchiness and tremendously irritable effort.

At this point, I realize that except during my pregnancies, this is the longest I've ever gone without alcohol. And even though I can't remember the last time I felt this awful, I'm proud that I'm starting something I'm sure is healthy.

In the car on the way home from a weekend meeting, I pull over to the side of the road and call my mom. She's the first person I tell about what I've been doing. She's been sober twenty-four years and knows something about alcoholism, but it's still difficult for me to admit what's been going on.

When I make up my mind to stay sober and live without alcohol, I realize the extent to which it has me. A friend of mine compares alcohol to a fishhook. It's only when you try and pull away that you realize the damn thing is digging deeper into your cheek and that you're doomed—trapped in a way much more extensive than you ever imagined.

The symptoms of physical withdrawal feel like drowning. I can't catch my breath. I am full of panic at the thought of doing even basic things like picking up my girls from school. And I get sick several times in succession with strep. When I call to talk to my sponsor about it, she tells me people trying to get sober often get sick a lot. It feels like my body is calling my bluff: "Now let's see what you got, Fancy Pants!" My early days are filled with high temperatures, trips to the doctor, and hours spent on the couch. My husband misses tons of work covering for me, and my kids watch hours of *Dora* and *Diego*. Some people get sober and get their lives together. I get sober and fall completely apart. So I follow instructions and take it slowly. One minute at a time.

The only skill I need in the beginning is the ability to pick up the phone and tell someone that I feel

Mommy Doesn't Drink Here Anymore

like drinking and to steer clear of alcohol in all its lovely guises: no trips to the grocery store, or restaurants, no eye contact with my beautiful drink that I love. One foot in front of the other, trudge, trudge, trudge. Very slowly, I start to follow the instructions I'm given. I try to eat balanced meals at regular times and follow routines. At first, I don't understand how sharing a healthy family meal in the evening helps keep me sober. I have long protested domestic drudgery, which when you're a parent, makes about as much sense as falling into an icy cavern while championing your refusal to use your crampons to arrest your descent. The ritual of eating together proves very comforting to all of us, especially since Mommy no longer has wine as her security blanket. Very early on, I begin to remember how lovely little rituals can be.

Early sobriety also means admitting that I cannot do this by myself. Asking for help becomes an exercise in humility and helps me drop the pose that I am independent and bulletproof. But these calls aren't about slogging around in sorry stew. They are about seeking guidance regarding the next right step. Rather than seeking out coconspirators and sympathizers, I am taught to reach out in order to get real, constructive help, not to keep the slog alive. I learn that there are no real solutions in drama-land, only runny mascara and long go-nowhere missives to the universe, essentially all asking the same question: *Why do all these hard things keep happening to me?*

If you're willing to ask for help and actually want it, it is an entirely different exercise, one with a real possibility of a hopeful outcome, one that promises something productive to happen as a result. Sympathy might play a part in the exchange, but only as a mechanism of bolstering your intention rather than purposeless jawing.

A few days pass as my commitment to sobriety takes shape and solidifies. I feel like I've signed up for some kind of spiritual boot camp, and in a way I have.

CHAPTER 6

30 days and beyond: swearing is my higher power

I pick my sponsor because she is beautiful and kind. She is fresh faced and long legged and gorgeous, the kind of woman men love to stare at from under their caps. You're supposed to pick someone who has something you want. Wise counsel. When she walks in, you can almost hear all the held in wolf whistles and sense the testosterone-taming self-discipline all the 12-Step people require to stay seated. You can see them telling themselves to calm the freak down. She's also funny and charming and swears like a trucker. I really admire that in a woman.

In addition to being utterly lovely, she's tough talking, open, and forthright, and talks about her wonderful marriage, all the while sharing her stories of how alcohol brought her to her knees repeatedly: her multiple relapses, near suicide, and pill addiction. When I tell her I have to drink, *have to,* she really understands. She shares her stories of hiding wine/liquor/pills everywhere, how she nearly lost everything, her life, her beloved husband, and her will to live.

They make a big deal in 12-Step meetings about how each of us gets to decide who our Higher Power (or God) is. This is very helpful to many of us who come in and can't even remember our names, let alone who or what or if God or Goddess or anyone is. There is a guy in my noon meeting who calls his higher power Jake. When he talks about praying to Jake, I always peek around to see if anyone looks angry or judgmental, but usually all I see are smiles and nods, like, "Yes, yes, please go on." I don't really have a problem with God per se, having been a nice Mormon girl for a few years, but sometimes I like to joke that swearing is my Higher Power. Swearing is a silly thing to worship, but there's something about the bad words flying out of my mouth that feels cleansing and clarifying. Later, I decide that I should cut back on the f-bombs, but not for a while. It's still too fun. And I can't give up all my bad habits in one fell swoop, for heaven's sake.

One night, I call my sponsor and say I'm not sure how I'm going to make it from 5 to 8 P.M. without drinking my weight in wine, and she says, "How about I come over and we can talk about it? I hope it's okay that I'm in my pajamas." And then it becomes utterly clear (again) why men aren't allowed to sponsor women and vice versa. I laugh and tell her, "Of course! You realize, of course, that I'll probably have to drink later, but come on over anyway!"

And then she's at the door. I barely let her sit down before launching into the many great reasons I should be able to continue drinking. First, I wasn't really that bad. Second, I never had a DUI. Third, it's fun and everyone knows mothers hardly ever have fun. Fourth, I miss it so much I think I'm going to die.

She nods and smiles and suggests we play Scrabble. I love to play Scrabble, not as much as I love to drink, but it's all right as a distraction. As we play, she asks me to imagine the worst hangover I ever had. I think of the day I missed the twins' kindergarten open house because I was shaking and nauseous in the bathroom. She shares some delicious chocolate and something shifts and eases up. And before I know it, it is gone. That compulsion to drink something, anything to take me away.

Something about eating chocolate while talking hangovers with a hot woman in pajamas who's good at word games kicks that drinking demon right out of my house for one more evening.

So long, sucker!

I wake up the next morning feeling alert and un-hung over, and I think, "Well, I didn't drink last night," and then, "Maybe just one wouldn't hurt," but before that thought takes root, I go to another meeting and cry and talk about things I've hidden under rocks for so long. I'm like a little old woman sorting through a pile of worms, looking for a lost jewel, while the others nod and listen patiently.

Then some guy says, "Sometimes this program is all I have," and I start to cry because I know exactly what he means. And this moment of recognition wraps me again in solace, and I feel the broken places start healing. We're like people lifting up our shirts and sharing war wounds, all the while looking at each other lovingly and nodding our understanding. "Of course it hurts! Of course you drink. Of course you're lonely. Of course you need more love and support. You are home now. You are one of us." A statement that might make some recoil with rebellion fills me with a sense of belonging.

Mommy Doesn't Drink Here Anymore

As far as I'm concerned, alcohol is the ultimate bait and switch. Booze is suspiciously similar to the book my parents gave us when we were young called, "What Is Happening to Me?" that lures you in with colorful cartoon people who appear to be having fun but upon closer examination are really just kids changing into adults (with hair growing down there). Everywhere you look, there are naked body parts, and men and women in bed (What are they doing? They're making love!). The cartoons get you to open the cover, and before you can slam it shut, the images burn themselves on your brain.

Like the book from childhood, alcohol is the cartoon cover hiding the stark reality and bad news inside. My drink book is filled with friendly look-ing cartoons, accompanied by disturbing captions: "Here we see Mommy throwing up in the toilet after having two bottles of wine," and then "Mommy and Daddy try to make love sober now. Mommy doesn't like it without the wine." And the next page: "Here is Mommy eating a Snickers in the evening instead of having wine. She hopes she won't get a bigger arse, but likely she will." It's meant as a funny step-by-step but it's serious and at times overwhelming in its realism.

It becomes clear I'll need a little extra outside help if I'm going to make it through the mire of new sobriety, so I start seeing a therapist, who agrees to see me on Friday evenings, a time previously devoted to drinking. So much of new sobriety is developing replacement activities and rituals, and it is lovely to add Friday evening therapy to my growing list of "things to do other than drink." For 90 minutes, we talk about sobriety, marriage, and whether or not I'm having a midlife crisis. He likes to remind me that people die from alcoholism. This is irritating, especially since I enjoy joking around about it. I guess he's got a point. I hate that he doesn't fall for my clever repartee, but I also admire him for it. If conning therapists is worthy of a medal, I usually bring home the gold. As I talk to him week after week, I slowly feel better. Less twitchy, less manic, less like I need to perform. We discuss the merits of sobriety, coolly and rationally, but he always comes back to the fact that if I keep drinking I'll die. I try and make that funny somehow, but death by drinking is tough to joke about, especially since I know people whose loved ones have died from alcoholism.

Other things stop being funny too, but maybe I was never really laughing anyway. Maybe I was poking fun, being cruel, making light in order to focus attention away from the sinking vessel of my life. There is a better, kinder laughter woven into meetings, laughter born of recognition rather than cynicism and snark. It is joyful and playful and healing. There is no one-upmanship in it, only warmth and a collective sigh of relief that we don't have to do this alone anymore. Life can get better for us, one day at a time.

But without the comforting familiarity of snark, cynicism, and wine, I'm like a jellyfish, stranded on a beach, flopping around wondering if this is all the fun there is left to have. I'm a woman of extremes. If I get healthy, will there be anything saucy left? I'm turning forty this year, and I'm not sure I'm ready to call the game for the healthy team. Yes, I can't drink anymore (probably), but must I give up on all my other dreams of living in Paris or London? Traveling the world? Hurried intellectual conversations and hot passion on the floor? Are these things now replaced by me sitting in a smelly room full of drunks, laughing over how we all fall into the same big pit? Probably.

I am not drinking anymore. I repeat it to myself over and over until I almost mean it, but it doesn't sink in. It feels like pretending. I say "No thank you" to the ghosts in my head. I go to meetings every day, sometimes twice, and try to avoid the rhythms of my old habit, like being alone with the kids without a plan in the afternoon and evening—or the end of the day, when we're all tired and hungry, when they've wiped the floor with me and what I need more than oxygen or water is quiet and rest, but there won't be any rest or quiet for hours and hours. These are the hours of my drinking. And now these are the hours when I practice breathing and reading and resting and talking to 12-Step pals and my therapist instead.

Until getting sober, I never countered my kids' unending demands on my time or energy with healthy boundaries. I'd never say, "Hey kids, give me 5 minutes of quiet, I'm exhausted," or "You are not allowed to wake me up at 2 A.M. just because you want to tell me something." I simply complied with most of their desires and drank the feelings of exhaustion and resentment away. Around 11 A.M. I'd plan for the evening's supply by calling my husband and pretending we needed legitimate groceries like bread or milk, and then casually throw in, "Oh and could you pick up a couple of bottles of wine?" as if he didn't know what I was playing at. Without alcohol, it is unclear how this whole family machinery will get from point A to point B—how I will get from noon to 8 P.M. every day. Without my favorite shortcut, I need to come up with a different plan, one that involves asking for help and admitting when I'm down for the count. After all, it takes a special kind of insanity to pick a fight with a time of day. I think it will require something creative to resolve the conflict. I am wrong. It is the very simple and often dull things that get me through (eating balanced meals, talking to friends, taking baths, reading, watching movies, and writing all become great distractions that develop into wonderful rituals).

And though it's counterintuitive to give up the padding in the machinery of my afternoons, I know that if I start drinking again I'll be right back to square one, which will be a drag since I'll have to admit it out loud to my home group, my sponsor, and my family. If what I've done to this point in adulthood hasn't worked very well, it's time to try someone else's ideas on for size. I get most of my instructions from the meetings, but some of them come directly from my sponsor. I have to get rid of all the booze and all my exposure to it. It is important to start telling everyone I know that I'm not drinking anymore. If there are get-togethers or barbecues, I bring my own nonalcoholic drinks. If we are hosting, we don't serve alcohol. People are generally very understanding and accommodating. A few are offended when asked not to bring alcohol, but they get over it, or at least keep it to themselves.

It helps immensely that my work schedule is flexible, so I am able to devote a fair amount of time to attending meetings and talking with others on the same path. Of course, we're also putting groceries on credit, have no retirement, tons of debt, and are in considerable financial trouble. From a balance sheet perspective, I need to get myself into a full-time job. From another view, I'll lose everything if I can't figure out how to live without alcohol. I'm highly doubtful I'll be able to do all this if I don't have the time to go to meetings.

I've heard people say that staying busy early in sobriety is absolutely necessary. One woman tells the story of how her first sponsor told her to paint the outside of her house those first few months. Most working parents are already bountifully blessed with busyness—frenetic activity and exhaustion, more like. And I find this busyness clarifying. If I focus on what is at hand—making dinner, helping with shoes, breaking up fights—time goes more quickly. If I start daydreaming about how lovely it used to be, using alcohol as my time machine, time slows to a crawl.

Each evening, I put the girls to bed between 7 and 8 P.M. and then go to bed myself, not to sleep, but to read, watch movies, or talk on the phone to someone else in the program. And one other small semiembarrassing thing: I eat candy.

The floor around my bed looks like rejected wrappers from the board game Candy Land, like a sugary stairway out of Hell's half-acre. Candy is something to look forward to, candy and quiet and rest. On any given day, my nightstand drawer is full of Runts, Hot Tamales, Whoppers, Junior Mints, and peanut butter cups.

Surprisingly, I don't blow up to 800 pounds. Maybe it's not so surprising, considering the thousands of daily alcohol calories that have been my wont. I'm surprised to find that, after a while, this evening ritual is almost as good as drinking myself into oblivion. Or at least it's an acceptable substitute. I'm a bon vivant, and I've taken to my bed. It's funny and kind of laughable, but it works.

I think of all those ladies in Edith Wharton novels taking to bed with headaches or mystery ailments brought on by tight corsets and even tighter social conventions, and I think they are definitely on to something. Or maybe Stuart Smalley is a better guide for me, looking in the mirror saying I like myself. Whether I'm modeling myself after a fictitious nineteenth-century character or a 12-Step *Saturday Night Live* character with low self-esteem doesn't really matter. Little by little, alcohol's death grip loosens.

Mommy Doesn't Drink Here Anymore

I don't think of it every 30 seconds. I can go 5, sometimes 10, minutes without obsessing. I still long for alcohol and dream of drinking and wish I could live in ignorance of what ails me. I watch with keener eyes the goings-on in my household. I threaten. I cajole. I grieve for all that I've missed. I am furious by turns at myself and then the twins' dad and then my husband. Blaming, self-flagellating, blaming again. I'm an angry emotional woman, and I pity those who live with me during this first part of sobriety. For better or for worse makes sense about now.

But there is also laughter. Not at home, not yet, but in meetings. We laugh together over the things we used to tell ourselves about how we didn't have a problem with alcohol. We laugh about broken marriages, broken promises, DUIs, and drug busts. It isn't funny in the way that sometimes you feel like giggling in church or a funeral (because you know you shouldn't). We laugh the way you do with a friend who understands the exact colors and textures of your pain and struggles, around whom you can relax and feel understood.

When someone understands your particular brand of angst, both of you are freed up to have more humor, more knowledge, and less tragedy. In this off-kilter way, you help each other see things clearly. In meetings, we laugh over what a mess it all is. We cry too, but it's the laughter that keeps me coming back. I've never sat inside such gales of laughter before, and I can feel my broken heart healing an hour at a time.

I remember being a flutist in college, sitting in the middle of the orchestra as we played Aaron Copeland's *Appalachian Spring,* feeling enveloped in the surging music. The melody rich and power-ful, layered with low and high notes; first strings, then percussion, then woodwinds, and then brass. I remember closing my eyes waiting for my part and feeling so moved, so lucky to be in that place at that moment sitting right in the middle of the heartbeat of the orchestra. Laughing in meetings feels just like that. I can laugh or not, but just to be surrounded by this deep understanding and accepting laughter is like sitting in the middle of a well-tuned orchestra, all of us playing our parts, some dubious, some skeptical, and some wholly embracing the chaos and beauty of it all.

The day I take my 30-day coin, my mother and sponsor and husband sit next to me. It feels like such an auspicious day, the end of the 30 longest days of my life. They ask if anyone has 30 days of continu-ous sobriety, and I proudly walk to the front to take the bright red coin. This group of people has become a welcoming comforting community—the first real community to which I've ever belonged. We're held together by mutual suffering and a wholehearted commitment to overcome our common addiction, to have a collective thought that we might not have to drink again. And sometimes, rather than depressing the hell out of me, this thought makes me smile.

Mommy Doesn't Drink Here Anymore

CHAPTER 7

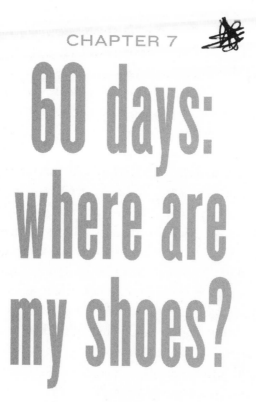

60 days: where are my shoes?

I am terrified of having sex sober. It's been a long, long time, and I'm convinced it is going to be horrid. My husband and I are barely speaking. If it's not about the kids or dinner or the checking account, or work, we're not talking about it. Even though he's very supportive of my sobriety and rarely raises an eyebrow at how much of my time this is all taking (he did, after all, notice the ten-bottle pileup in the recycling bin when I was drinking), he can't help but notice that I'm more interested in cleaning toilets than I am in getting physical. Suddenly, the unhappiness is palpable, no longer drowned out by the drinking and denial.

Furthermore, as the fog begins to lift, I am even more lost than before: an earthquake survivor wandering around squinting at rescuers' name tags, wondering what happened to my shoes. I look and feel like hell and hope that soon the Magic will happen, capital M. The fabulous bucket of luck that pours down onto the heads of hardworking souls trying valiantly to be good and give up the booze and the swearing.

Isn't it obvious that people like me deserve amazingly good things to happen in one week, or maybe two, tops? Things like finding our one true love, winning the lottery, or having a very distant relative die and leave us a huge house in Tuscany?

On the contrary. The fog lifts, and I wake up to the train wreck that is my life.

Even with my hesitation about our physical relations, I still feel squirmy and jumpy, like if I don't get laid soon I'm going to start eating dirt or chewing on leather straps. I close my eyes tightly and try very hard not to notice the cute guys with the many years of sobriety and the tight jeans. Instead, I shake my head to clear the images. And repeat my new mantra: *I will stay married just for today.* For today, I can do this.

It's hard for a harlot to get sober.

Getting sober is like getting a cavity drilled without the anesthetic, but not quite that bad, since I am usually in a room full of people also getting their teeth drilled without drugs, many of whom can make me belly laugh about the stupidity of it all. Why is saying stuff out loud like "I used to drink two bottles of wine a day and didn't think I had a problem" soooo funny? I have no idea, but it's the closest thing to Magic I've ever experienced, and if anyone ever says, "Magic," I almost always roll my eyes.

I've never laughed or cried this hard or loudly. But the crying (my crying, anyway) gets really annoying after a while. It's usually not cute weepy and quiet, it's snorky and snotty and gaggy. This is the kind of sobbing I used to keep neatly hidden inside my therapist's office or confined to late-night arguments with my spouse, long before I learned the very unhealthy but effective advantage of stuffing everything way deep down inside.

Soon I begin looking around and seeing the other people in the meetings. By accident or grace, I pick a chair next to a man 20 to 40 years my senior (age is hard to pinpoint when people like to drink and take drugs, thereby aging themselves way beyond their chronological years) who'd been in and out of sobriety for thirty years. Ted and I came into the program within a week of each other, and that creates a strong bond between us. Plus, he's cranky and unfriendly in the most familiar way. I have always agreed with curmudgeons.

When I first meet Ted, he sits with his eyes glued to the floor, wearing a cap and dark shades. He wears an Army jacket and carries a walking stick, and after he realizes that I'm going to keep sitting by him and joshing him before meetings, he starts calling me "Sweetie" and notices when I'm not there. We sit together for a few weeks before we share a few more details, and pretty soon when we take a coin, we nod at each other and place the coin in each others' hands for a blessing. And we become friends.

About three months into our camaraderie, I see his blue eyes for the first time. One day, he takes off his dark shades and removes his cap. If you've never made eye contact with someone you've spent time around and then you do, you know what I mean. It was shocking and personal. Not a lovey-dovey gaze, but a "Hey I see you!" kind of experience. Amazing. When you go to the same meeting every day and sit in the same seat, you have a different experience of the passage of time. It slows down for that hour, and slowly you become part of something, maybe for the first time in your life. Knowing that Ted will be in his spot holds me to the group. If I'm too tired to go to a meeting, I think of him, and I'm shaken out of my lethargy.

The first time Ted doesn't show up for a meeting, I worry and fret but hope he is just at a doctor's appointment or visiting his son. After another few days go by and still no Ted, I call his cell phone and a robot voice reports it's no longer in service. A week later he shows up wrecked. His dark glasses and hat are back on, and he stares at the carpet for the longest time. I sit down and give him a hug and ask him where in the hell he's been. We both know the answer: he's relapsed. He says he's here today because he's decided he wants to live. I put my hand on his shoulder and realize he's my lifeline. And I can't stop crying. If he's chosen to live, we can go on from here. Without him, I feel worried and scared and alone. He's back now, and we're going to keep sitting together and doing this thing together. We're a team. You're not supposed to wrap your sobriety around someone else, but I can't help feeling that ours is connected. I see him again and feel okay, like you feel okay when you stop breathing and then start again, like when you think the world is going to end and then it doesn't.

It is unnerving how many people come in and say they want to quit drinking and then never return. Out of five new people or so a week, maybe one or two are still there one month later. The group becomes tightly knit, mostly because we're a shipwrecked crew on a lifeboat trying to keep the others on board, sometimes forcing them to grab the ring, other times turning away from all their determined drowning. As time marches on and I near 60 days without a drink, I know people's names and whether they drink regular or decaf coffee, whether they have children or grandchildren, whether they work or are retired, and how long they've been sober. We celebrate annual sobriety birthdays, and I slowly realize that many of the people in this group have been sober ten years or more. (In my 12-Step group, we celebrate increments of continuous sobriety: 30 days, 60 days, 90 days, 6 months, 9 months, 1 year, and every year after that. We call these "birthdays.") Of course when you first see a sixty-year-old celebrating his 20th birthday, it can be a bit confusing. To help with this, 12-Steppers refer to their actual birthdays as "belly button" birthdays. Before trying to get sober, I'd never imagined this was the sort of enterprise one continued working on after a year or two. The old-timers tell me that quitting drinking is only the beginning, but between 30 and 60 days sober quitting drinking is absolutely enough work for now. I go to at least one meeting a day, and it has slowly made a huge difference in my life.

In the land between 30 and 60 days, I also consider whether or not I should file for divorce. I feel like someone has come into my house and stolen away all the love I used to have for this man and replaced it with a heart shot full of Novocain. In a sense, I'm right. Alcohol has covered it up, with my aiding

Mommy Doesn't Drink Here Anymore

and abetting, and filled our house with mistrust and anger and accusation. I talk with my sponsor, and she shares the general wisdom that it is best not to make any life-altering decisions in the first year of sobriety. I argue and bargain, but she smiles and tells me to just take it one day at a time. After a while, things at home get so tense (too many arguments, kids not sleeping well, everyone on edge) that Jack and I decide to take some time apart. He agrees to stay at our camping trailer and cool off for a few days.

The challenges of the first year of sobriety, especially within the family, cannot be overstated. How have I let things go this long without calling an end to them? I stay because I think it is the best thing for the kids and possibly even for me. I stay because I want to be a good mother. I want to keep our family together, but I'm not sure I can.

It is a few days before Thanksgiving, and my husband's father and stepmom are coming into town for a visit. It's a recipe for a grim little holiday: separated spouses, scared children, in-laws, and new shaky sobriety. We manage to muddle through, and it's the first Thanksgiving in years that I don't drink all the livelong day. There is a chapter in the Big Book that talks about what happens to the family after one of the adults sobers up. It's not pretty, and even though it's written from the standpoint of *Father Knows Best* and wives who stand by their men after years of heavy drinking, it speaks to me. I look around our holiday table and start noticing what has been going on here.

The kids are nervous and tentative around their step-father; he and I say nothing to each other; and his parents are trying not to step on all the land mines everywhere. It's like sitting in a room with everyone wearing their clothes inside out . . . We see the tags, the hems, the wrinkles, and we try and laugh and talk around it, all the while hoping that everything will be okay.

Over the holiday weekend, I try explaining to the kids in very general terms that Mommy doesn't drink anymore and that I need to go to meetings to help me be a better mother. They take it at face value and their play begins to incorporate "going to meetings to learn about being a good mama." They're only five, five, and two, so this is more than sufficient for the cause. Their stepfather comes home for dinner and tucks them in every night, but then he goes away.

Once they figure out this is happening, they watch the window like hawks and wail and cry for him when he drives away. It's heartbreaking. In the end, I give in and ask him to move back home. I can't see how me not being in love anymore and him occasionally los-ing his temper is sufficient cause to break up our little family, at least not at this juncture. I tell him if he lays one hand on the kids I will divorce him immediately. He takes this seriously and agrees to get counseling. There is some improvement and then more as time goes on. After awhile, I feel safe leaving him for short periods of time alone with the girls. But it is still so broken, our marriage. I'm doubtful it can ever recover.

Knowing what I know about divorce and children and adults who are ignorant of their children's suffering, how can I bear to rip my own children apart from the only family unit they've ever known? I simply cannot. At least not today.

These thoughts bring me back to now. Right where I'm standing. And going to meetings and working with others start to bring relief from these brain fevers, this guilt and shame. There are no answers, and nothing strikes me as the answer except this: I need to get clearer. And to do that, to achieve some sort of higher-order spiritual cleansing and insight into the complex problems of my adult life, I need to stay sober. If I drink, I'll be right back in the mud pit of confusion and misery.

It is breathtakingly difficult to stand here without a painkiller and face the demons of my choices, but I start to believe the only way through is through. I hear people talk about learning to love, learning to believe in a Higher Power; I see others go in and out of the program, irritated by the 12-Step God talk, but really just want to stop drinking. What I now believe is that I'll never have any answer to these dilemmas, I'll never grow and change and learn what I need to learn unless I stop drinking. More specifically, I'll never know if I should stay married unless I stay sober.

For the first time it occurs to me that my best chance of finding and providing happiness and stability for myself and my children is to stay sober and work a program of recovery. If I follow a proven road map rather than my own, maybe we all have a good chance of achieving some kind of wholeness. But the time between now and then seems insurmountably long. Without love, sex, and passion between us, my husband and I have nothing at home but work and kids and kids and work.

Despite all this, as 30 days becomes 60 without a drink, I find myself less tied up in knots about what will happen and more concerned with the here and now. And while I'm not particularly happy and serene, I start to feel moments of peace. Moments of silence and calm, like maybe just maybe everything might work out just fine. And for a girl like me who has always had more spice than milk, more hope than happiness, this is downright miraculous.

And something else: I start really seeing my children, not as just very hungry small adults, or hellions whom I love, or things that happened on my way to growing up. I start thinking they're funny and charming and likeable. I don't block out their noise and conversation and imagine drinking wine on a boat with an Italian lover. Instead, I look into their eyes and converse about important things like birds and worms and clouds. And it's not dramatically more interesting than it ever was, but I'm listening and hearing and I'm not numbed out. Sometimes when they fight and scream, it's punishing, but mostly it's very good. We play together and enjoy one another's company. We make up songs and talk about what we will do today.

Mommy Doesn't Drink Here Anymore

I've sat in meetings with parents who've had their children taken away because of drugs and alcohol, parents who sober up once their kids leave home, parents who have missed out on what I have. And I'm grateful to have a chance to be present and sober for their lives while they're still young. I'm grateful and hopeful and walk toward 60 days starting to believe that I've finally turned things around. That whatever else happens, I've saved my children from being motherless, orphans of alcohol and oblivion and distraction. I may not be able to give them a home with a happy marriage or a healthy relationship, but I've given them a mother who can change and learn to love them, learn to like them deeply, eye to eye, nose to nose.

More than anything else, I don't want to miss out on the good parts of raising kids. The tantrums, nighttime wakefulness, and sassy pants routines, I could do without. Alas, life is at my beck and call, customizable to my every whim. One of the challenges of early sobriety is coming up with activities to enjoy as a family that don't center around drinking alcohol. Putting down the computer and the wineglass are the first step. But following that, we slowly begin to develop new ways to relate:

⭐ **Bike rides around the neighborhood.**
They ride. I walk and assist.
⭐ **Nature walks.** We live near a forested land trust, and the kids enjoy collecting leaves and

pretending we're lone adventurers discovering secret passageways.

⭐ **Baking.** We bake cookies or banana bread together. I wouldn't have previously had the patience for this, but now it's okay as long as expectations are kept low.

⭐ **Swimming.** We swim during the summer mostly, but we've taken advantage of the family hour at the local swimming pool as well.

⭐ **Soccer.** Organized sports provide a wonderful excuse to sit outdoors and relax while the kids are engaged in muscle- and spirit-building activities.

I am rightly wary of family activities that used to revolve around drinking—eating out at restaurants, barbecues, Thanksgiving.

Sometimes I exist only for that hour each day with that group of people where I feel safe, where I can be myself, and where I never have to find people's socks and get them snacks (well, hardly ever). The hour each day that starts helping me believe that there just might be a way out.

A way out for all of us, no matter how much we've lost.

Mommy Doesn't Drink Here Anymore

CHAPTER 8

90 days: so this is life

I can sit still for an hour. When I sit in my seat now, I can do so with only minimal shifting around and leg shaking. I still crane my neck as people walk in and out, secretly peep at the occasionally cute guys who come in here, but I start living for the coins (awarded at increments of sobriety), the pretty, shiny colors, the applause, and the progress. At three months, the withdrawals and total freaked-out weirdness start to subside, but in their place is not magic, or money, or jobs. In their place is a cold, hard, dry land where the water lies deep below the surface and survival is possible only for those strong enough to dig with spoons.

When I first decide to stop drinking, I am not sure if I am a real alcoholic, but by 3 months sober I am no longer questioning, not very often anyway. I just know that I am. The stories I hear, the ones I share, the way I see what alcoholism does if people keep drinking, all the brokenness and healing is all the evidence I need. I am an alcoholic. When my stepmother comes along with me to one of my meetings, I introduce myself as an alcoholic and she cries. I think she's relieved and glad I'm here. She tells me later that it is sad to hear an adult child admit she's alcoholic, and I think she must be right. Wouldn't it be sad if your child admitted she had a problem with drinking? Or would it be sadder if he kept his drinking hidden away, in laundry baskets, cupboards, and garages? Obviously, I think the latter. Despite all my shame, I'm proud to call myself an alcoholic because I'd rather be something real than hide away any longer and pretend everything is just fine when it isn't, when it hasn't been okay for years.

Every week, a group of young women from a treatment center for teen girls visit my home group. They look so young and sweet and innocent, but their stories of abuse and addiction are chilling. When I look at them, I see my daughters. I wonder what will happen to my sweet girls if they start to have problems with alcohol. I review what I'll tell them *(Given your family history with alcohol, you'd be wise to skip it all together)*, walk through our imaginary first conversation when they admit they're curious about drinking. I try not to freak out as I calmly explain that what they decide to do at a certain age is their choice, but that while they are at home, I don't want them drinking. And then I start to panic. But the teens' presence at our weekly meetings always ends up more comforting than troubling. I look over at the young, fresh faces of the girls visiting from treatment, and I realize that at least my daughters will have somewhere to turn. Maybe they'll be able to be saved.

I used to pray to God when I found myself in a pinch of some kind. Prayer was like playing the lottery and hoping to win. I knew someone (probably God or Jesus) knew the numbers; they just had to give them to me and all would be well. Then all the problems would disappear, replaced by dancing fairies and obedient children and meaningful remunerative work. And did I mention I would also begin to look like the after pictures in those makeover shows? Just magically, by not drinking, my skin would glow, my hair would be silky and long, and my angelic countenance would melt the hearts of sober, attractive, self-sacrificing men everywhere.

At 3 months sober, I finally feel like I just might make it to my one-year sobriety date. But everything else is falling apart quickly. My job contract ends, and we face immediate shortfalls in our monthly budget. We've decided to put our house on the market, but no one has made any offers. Meanwhile, we've gone to marriage counseling, and we're more stuck than ever. I feel done. But can I face another ruined relationship? Can I bear to make another deposit in my children's therapy fund?

I remember our last marriage counseling session clearly. Our counselor is very wise and friendly, and she asks us each to identify what our overarching goal is for the marriage. He says, "Stay together." I say, "Be happy." And then she sits and smiles at us knowingly. "Well, my first suggestion is for you both to find a way to identify a common goal. Obviously staying together and being happy are not always the same thing." Obviously. When the counselor probes us for more information, Jack goes into a litany of all of my faults, mistakes, and ways I've done him wrong. That he is nearly 100% accurate on all counts only makes me madder. At one point he volunteers, "If she is really serious about her sobriety, she'll stay married to me." A clever tie-in. He knows I'm far more committed to my sobriety at this point than to staying married. And I want to kick him in the shins. Instead, I walk out of our appointment and call my sponsor. To my complaints she answers, predictably, "Rachael, I understand why you are upset and why Jack pisses you off. I'd be angry right now too. But your sobriety is more important than your anger. So please, just go to a meeting, pray, and then call me again later."

And once again, I follow her very wise counsel. And the day ends better than it starts.

I've had all these years to do things my way, to mixed effect. I am thoroughly ready to follow instructions from others who have kicked alcohol and found happiness. If that means that for today I don't file for divorce, then so be it.

CHAPTER 9

6 months: marital openings

All of a sudden the freight train rushing through my brain every two seconds screaming out, "Drink, drink, chugga, chugga, drink, drink!" is quiet like a little bunny, soft as a whisper.

Except when it isn't.

My husband Jack comes to see me collect my 6-month coin. This does not fill me with joy. It feels as if my sacred chamber has been sullied with the outside world. Or, more accurately, someone who knows what a total asshole I can be is coming into a place where I usually manage to be patient and kind. I hope he'll keep this knowledge to himself.

"Welcome. Is there anyone here in their first 30, 60, or 90 days of continuous sobriety? How about 6 months?"

I raise my hand. "I'm Rachael and I'm an alcoholic, and today I have 6 months."

Applause.

I head up to the front of the room to collect my coin. I hug the chairperson and then sit back down between Ted and Jack. Ted gets the coin, not Jack, since Ted is my sober-mate, here for me day in and day out, armed with his camouflage hat, walking stick, and candy bars.

The chair asks, "Rachael, do you have a topic?"

And then I imagine how it could go very, very wrong. . . .

Jack raises his hand.

"Excuse me. I'm glad Rachael is finally sober and every-thing and you all have helped her stay off the wine, but you

have no idea what she's really like to live with. She's hostile, self-absorbed, and completely cold to me. She's sweet to the kids but no one else. . . ." An uncomfortable silence fills the room, as my safe haven becomes my tribunal.

Luckily, this isn't how it happens.

I am asked to pick the topic, and I mumble something about gratitude and then, "I can't believe I've been coming here nearly every day for half a year. Only half a year ago I couldn't go longer than 48 hours without a drink. If you'd have told me 6 months ago that this day would ever come, I'd have thought you were insane."

Everyone nods, and Jack puts his hand on my knee.

He asks to speak, and I cringe.

"I just want to thank each of you for being here for Rachael. She's relied on you and this program. And we're both incredibly grateful for your kindness." He is teary-eyed and humble, and everyone pats him on the back. At which point I immediately start resenting his presence. I don't want him thanking them, my people, and my sponsor, for getting me through.

And so I sit and shake my leg and listen halfheartedly to the other people talking about gratitude. And even in this defiant, irritable state, I know I'll feel better after the meeting. And I do.

At 6 months sober I feel like a bastardized version of that Sam Cooke song, "Wonderful World":

Don't know much about ~~history~~ love or marriage
Don't know much ~~biology~~ about intimacy

Don't know much about ~~a science book~~ being happy
Don't know much about ~~the french I took~~ staying married
But I do know that ~~I love you~~ I can't drink
And I know that ~~if you love me too~~ if I don't pick up a drink
What a wonderful world this would be.

In the early days of my sobriety, when I see people collect coins for 6 months of sobriety, I look at them like they are the Buddha or Jesus or a Person with Knowledge of the Great Mysterious Happiness. I perceive a beatific smile and inner glowing knowledge that will be mine if I stay sober that long. For someone unable to stop drinking for even a week, six months seems like years. Surely, anyone with that much time must be completely enlightened.

In truth, at half a year in, I am only a smidgen clearer about my problems, and I haven't been magically granted the gift of insight when it comes to love. I am still not particularly happy or joyous or free (as the 12-Step saying goes), nor have I figured out my marriage, but I'm happier than I was and I'm not as obsessed with alcohol. And that seems miraculous. The 6-month coin looks beautiful on my key fob, and it feels like one hell of an accomplishment, even though being awake to my own imperfections is at times awfully discouraging.

In an effort to figure out where I've gone wrong, I frequently bend my friends' ears about their relationships: What makes them work? Why do they fail? I've pondered and poked and prodded. Only

Mommy Doesn't Drink Here Anymore

now am I catching a distant glimmer of what is wrong with my marriage. For a long time, I think I'm just missing whatever gene that makes people good at long-term committed relationships. When people say, "Marriage is hard work," I always assume they mean fighting over bills, or career, or in-laws, nothing as deep and unsettling as falling out of love or questioning the whole fabric of commitment. When people tell me, "Keep working at it, it will get easier," I smile and nod, but I secretly go on believing they can't understand the depths of my alienation and loneliness. At 6 months sober I begin seeing the connection between getting sober and staying married. Both are a choice, a daily choice, and both require tossing the idea that I am so unique and special in my struggle that no one can possibly understand. If I am wrong about my drinking, how many other things might I be wrong about? Perhaps there is more to learn yet.

During this time, I read Rebecca Woolf's memoir of her son's first year, *Rockabye: From Wild to Child,* and something clicks for me. A few weeks after bringing her baby home, she and her husband have it out over their mutual frustrations and difficulties as new parents. At one point, she tells him she feels totally trapped, and he retorts that he thinks they should just give their baby up for adoption. And this is honestly the first time I've ever experienced someone writing the words I've spoken to myself as a new mother: words of loneliness, alienation, and despair.

She and her husband work it out, whereas I left my twins' father after just such a conversation.

And it occurs to me that my struggles for lust and passion, happy children and a stable home life, and my rebellion against monogamy and commitment aren't even remotely unusual. They might not be common, but perhaps they're not as unacceptable as I think they are. What a relief!

★ ☆ ☆

A few weeks later, Jack invites me along on a business trip. It's all expenses paid to a waterfront hotel in Seattle, and I imagine lounging around in a robe on Sunday morning, drinking coffee and reading the paper. Nothing seems as rapturous after having kids. Well, almost nothing.

And that other thing is what makes me hesitate. I haven't been overly anxious to test out my sobriety + sex = nightmare theory, and Jack has been incredibly patient. Until now. Recently, he has begun wondering aloud whether this is a new lifestyle choice or whether I might warm up to him again. I honestly can't say. But I simply can't turn down the chance to get away for the night without kids, so I agree to come along later that evening.

On my way into the city, he calls and checks in, and we chat for a while and then he says, "Hey. I just want you to know I have dinner plans tonight."

"Ohhhhhhh?" I say, all evil come-into-my-lair-pretend-nicey nice.

"And who are you having dinner with?"

"Oh, just this woman I used to work with. Well, actually, she's someone who interned with us last year," he says, starting to sound somewhat nervous.

"So what. She's eighteen?"

"Actually she's twenty-three."

"Oh well, that's fine. I've already made other plans anyway. We can meet up after dinner." I act very cool and casual, but inside I'm a bit alarmed.

As we hang up, I pull off the highway to see if I can't drum up some other plans so that I'm not some chump wife waiting around in an expensive hotel room.

Later that evening, I'm back at the hotel room after having quick symbolic dinner with a friend (See? I have plans too!). Returning to the hotel room is a relief. My friend ordered a drink with dinner and it made me crazy. Besides, he's not particularly fascinated by what step I'm on or what I've learned from my sponsor. So there are a few lags in our conversation, and I claim a headache to get back to the fancy-view room and order up some chocolate mousse.

Around 11 P.M., Jack calls to report giddily that he's had a great night. A great dinner.

"Oh, I'm so glad. I'll see you when you get here," I chirp.

Right.

When he walks in, he's glowing. Wedding-day, just-got-a-job, lit-up-inside type of glowing. I feel jealous for a second, but then I'm happy for him. He starts talking away about his dinner, and I think this is perhaps the happiest I've seen him in three years. He's a little tipsy and quite chatty and checks in to ask if he might tell me about his evening. When I nod, he continues.

"We had a few glasses of wine and just enjoyed each other's company." And then more about what they talked about (politics and work) and what she's been up to since leaving Bellingham (big marketing firm).

I listen intently and then after a while he stops, looks at me, and smiles. "Hey! This is fun! You and I haven't talked like this for so long."

He's right. We haven't.

We never really dated, never really took the time to have carefree fun. Some of that is par for the course when one has children and marries a second time in one's mid-thirties. But some of it is that I've never been really very good at cutting loose and having fun. At least not without alcohol. I've also never had the gift of intimacy. Or maybe, since my sponsor will read this and pipe up with some sort of gentle correction, the issue is that I've always been too afraid, thus far, to give love a chance. Real adult love. I've always been too busy shaking in my shit-kicking boots, hiding behind swearing and emotional armor, to let anyone in very far. In the 12-Step group, I've learned that most of us are this scared inside. Some of us hide it better than others, but most of us are about ten years old—shy, broken, and waiting around for grace.

My name is Rachael, and I'm scared. And I'm soft. Underneath the swearing and the cynicism. You could break me like a pencil if you wanted to. Jack could break me like a pencil. And I hate him for that.

While Jack continues to recap his evening, all lit up like a kid on Christmas morning, I think something hopeful. Like a little glowworm sneaking into the evil, dark cortex of my cynical mind, this thought slides in:

I wonder if we could work this out. I wonder if I could find a way to love him again.

And for the first night in months, we look each other in the eye and laugh and talk like we have no other troubles in the world. Like there are no kids, no drinking problems, no illnesses or wars or disagreements or divorces. For one night, we pretend that we're happily married. And for one night I almost believe that we are.

CHAPTER 10

9 months and forty years

I turn forty this week. I am 9 months sober. I am an alcoholic. The co-occurrence of these experiences seems auspicious and weighty, but also a little goofy. Turning forty for some people signifies a great reason to buy a convertible or take on a lover, or get hair plugs, or act mature and dignified. For me, it means getting comfortable with being an alcoholic and attempting to find properly slimming underthings. I keep staring at myself in the mirror, trying to find evidence that I'll live on and on. My husband comes downstairs one morning and catches me studying my face.

"Hey there, beautiful, what are you doing?"

"Making sure I don't look forty."

"You don't. You look thirty-five."

"Thirty-five?!"

"Okay, thirty."

"That's better."

I warn him to be prepared for a week of crazy moodiness and total vanity. He makes a note of it and then offers to make me some coffee. I'm not sure I like how unfazed he seems by all this neurosis.

★ ☆ ☆

My friend Nan's sobriety date is one day later than mine, so she'll take her 9-month coin this week too.

We see each other on a sunny weekend morning before the 9 A.M. meeting.

"Hey, Nan!! You have 9 months!"

"Hey, Rachael! *You* have 9 months!" She hugs me and I hug her back and let her newly showered hair touch my face. I smile and hold her close. She always wears beautiful earrings and occasionally dazzles with some gorgeous blue eye shadow. One nice thing about seeing people every day—you get to study their style as well as their heart and soul.

We hook arms and walk into the meeting together.

Ted calls me later that day and asks when I'll be taking my coin. He takes the bus in to meetings and has some serious health problems that require many doctor appointments, so getting to and from meetings can be a big production.

"Thanks for checking with me, Ted. I'd really love for you to be there."

"Of course I'll be there, Sweetie."

And he is.

Every time I walk in and see Ted sitting in his seat (third from the back on the right-hand side of the room), I breathe more easily. I always see him first, sitting as he does with his back to the door, walking cane leaning against his chair, wearing a flannel shirt and his camouflage baseball cap.

On the day I take my 9-month coin, he's there. When they ask who has time and I raise my hand, I'm so proud I could burst. I go up to the front, get my hug, and then hand my coin to Ted. He smiles at me, puts his arm around me, and says, "I'm proud of you, Sweetie."

It's a grand day.

After the meeting, Ted pulls me aside and says he has something he has to tell me. He's shuffling around and looking down at his feet, just like the old days. I wait and then ask, "What is it, Ted?" I'm afraid he is going to tell me he drank again. I'm afraid he's going to tell me he's dying.

Instead, he puts his hand on my arm, looks directly into my eyes, and tells me he's moving away.

I feel the lump in my throat and look away long enough to croak out some fake good wishes. "It will be okay, Sweetie, we can still email," he tells me, but I'm not so sure. I turn to him and pretend to joke, "You know, Ted, I find this move of yours incredibly selfish. What about me? We were supposed to keep taking our time together!"

He knows I mean it. I put my head on his shoulder and breathe, fingers crossed, prayers sent to God or whomever: *Please keep him safe. Keep both of us sober.*

★ ☆ ☆

A few days later, I'm on a plane to San Francisco. When I hear the word *plane,* I immediately think of those little bottles of wine—so small and harmless. On a plane, you can drink for many good reasons— if you fake a fear of flying, you're just calming your nerves. Better yet, you can go to an airport bar and have a few first, so that by the time you're on the plane your glass or two won't have to be so rushed or desperate. Try twitching in your seat waiting for the cart to make it to you when you want a glass (no, a bottle) so badly you're on the border of yelling, "Come on, people!!"

Mommy Doesn't Drink Here Anymore

But you don't drink anymore.

Ah yes. That's right. I keep forgetting. So I'm flying sober on a plane to San Francisco to attend BlogHer, which if last year is any indication, is a hugely satisfying debauch peppered with cries of, "Hey! It's so nice to see you again!" and inspiring talks about monetizing your blog and doing good works. For me, it's like returning to the scene of the crime. Last year, I drank so much at this conference I was sick for three days straight upon my return. Needless to say, I plan to hit a few 12-Step meetings while I'm in town.

When I walk into the lobby, I'm carrying my 9-month coin tightly in my palm. I look around and recognize a few women. I immediately feel like I've swallowed something sharp and poisonous. . . . I duck into a booth and call my sponsor. I leave her a message: "Hey Jenny, it's me. Listen, I'm here in San Fran and it's beautiful, but I'm freaked out and the other ladies seem super-together and I'm not sure I can do this. Call me."

And then I take a breath, sit down, pretend to send some very important emails, and slowly feel better. One of the most healing things about this 12-Step program is that I am now in the habit of admitting the cracks in my veneer. To say something out loud like, "I'm nervous. I'm not sure I can do this," takes the pepper out of it and removes the shame.

I'm palling around with two of my writer girlfriends, Erin and Nell, who make me laugh and swear and feel like I'm on top of the world. One of them has been in recovery for years and the other doesn't drink, so they're both supportive of the whole 12-Step thing.

One evening we decide to brave the big cocktail party BlogHer is hosting at Macy's. We wander into a roped-off area, and all of a sudden there is a rushing noise and I realize it is the sound of a million women talking. It is so crowded that I keep bumping into people. There is a woman next to me who is holding a huge glass of white wine, and before I can turn away, she bumps me and some of the wine spills and suddenly I'm alert and shot through with adrenaline. I've sniffed my drug. And I'm off.

Dear God, I need a glass of wine. Just one to relax and unwind. Haven't I been good these past months? Don't I deserve it?

1-2-3-4-5-6-7-8-9-10. I count to myself.

In the crush and crowds, I've lost Erin and Nell, my sober beards. I've got to get out of here. I try and get to the food table, but in the line everyone is holding big fancy drinks with strawberries and limes and it all looks so delicious. And I'm so hungry and thirsty and tired. I need a sip of wine. A gulp. I need just a few minutes alone with a bottle.

Just a few won't hurt.

I run a few people over getting out of there. I am totally disoriented and can't see Nell or Erin anywhere.

I dial Erin's number. She picks up.

"Hey where are you guys? I'm trapped between 1,000 hooters and 800 margaritas. Help!"

Mommy Doesn't Drink Here Anymore

"We're over in fitness gear." She's laughing, and I can hear Nell in the background cracking jokes.

"Where is that? I'm totally turned around." I try to sound like I'm not a borderline cuckoo bird with nerves and the need to drink.

"Oh it's easy. Just head up the escalator—the north one—and we're right here on the third floor."

"Can you come get me?" Again, I try and sound less crazy than I actually feel.

"Rachael, is everything okay?"

"No. I'm frazzled and stressed, and I need you to come get me."

"We'll be right there. Stay right where you are."

"I'm standing in front of shoes."

"How appropriate. Hold on. We're coming."

I stare at the shoes and count to ten and breathe.

I turn around and see Erin smile and wave from the escalator she's coming down. Nell is right behind her and yells out, "Yo Red!" and I know I'm going to be okay.

We gather in our hotel room later the next day and get ready to say our good-byes. Nell calls me just as I'm boarding a double-decker bus for a tacky but wonderful tour of San Francisco. "Hey, Rachael. It was really nice spending time with you. What, are you crying over there? Relax, Red, I'm just saying thanks for coming."

"You too, Nell, I had the most fun. Maybe you can come visit me sometime."

I'm sitting on the top level of the bus and can touch the treetop next to us as the other people board.

I'm not hung over today. I'm so glad I didn't drink yesterday.

I say a little prayer of thanks. I'm 9 months sober and just turned forty. So this is life.

Later that day, when my flight lands and I enter the baggage claim area, I see all my daughters in matching pink party dresses, happy and bouncy, yelling, "Mama! Mama! Mama!" And if there is a more beautiful chorus, I have not yet heard it.

As Jack gets the luggage, I take the girls outside, and they race up and down on a dry patch of grass between walkways. It's a beautiful sunny evening, and I am the luckiest woman alive. And I think back to last year's trip. I spent nearly every evening at BlogHer '07 completely blitzed. I came home exhausted and hung over, with a high fever and strep throat. How lovely it is to be in recovery today! To come back home to see Jack's handsome face and the girls clamoring for hugs and to be present in this moment of sheer exultation, without guilt or shame or wondering what I did that I need to hide from Jack. A clear conscience is a beautiful thing.

Back home now, my sponsor and I discuss my marriage for the umpteenth time, and I worry she must be bored silly by the topic. We've discussed the possibilities ad nauseum: divorce, separation, raise the kids together but take lovers, get divorced but stay living in the same house, go to counseling, go away on a weekend, fake it until we make it. And I swear in this first year we've tried each possibility, but it

Mommy Doesn't Drink Here Anymore

usually comes down to this: I want to keep my family together no matter what. And for better or for worse, my family is Jack and the girls. He's spent more time with my daughters than almost anyone else. He has made great strides to improve his patience and understanding and has attended his own 12-Step group for people with loved ones in recovery.

And since I've tried every other thing and have a pretty good idea that taking this marriage a day at a time might work (it worked for the booze), I decide to give it a try.

CHAPTER 11

months 10
and 11:
high-bottom
girl

Occasionally, in topic meetings, someone chooses "your bottom" as the subject they'd like to discuss. I always feel sorry for the newcomer in times like these. The vernacular of 12-Step meetings is rife with double entendres. One of my little hobbies is to scan the room for newbies and try and elicit a giggle . . . or at least give them a wink and someone to feel saner than. Or I imagine all the fun I could have with various 12-Step terms and phrases:

Share about your bottom.

"Hi, I'm Rachael, and I have a very high bottom. And furthermore, my breasts are firm, my arms are toned, and I have abs of steel."

Have you had enough?

"Hi, I'm Rachael, and I can never ever have enough."

Remember your last drunk.

"He was totally hot. Tall, dark, and handsome."

The concept of a bottom, the spiritual or physical end of the line, the place people reach when they finally decide they're through with drinking or drugging, is a powerful one. Your bottom is whatever point at which you've had enough, whether you're under a bridge with a bottle in a bag or president of your own company. Your bottom is your bottom. And if this makes you laugh in a meeting, no doubt you'll not giggle alone. We are a twisted bunch.

Perhaps I am technically a high-bottom drunk—someone who didn't have to get arrested, or a DUI, or lose jobs—but I am a drunk nonetheless. I thought I didn't have any problem at all with alcohol until

I tried to stop drinking. Kind of like the dog who doesn't mind the muzzle until he tries to bark. All instinct. No reason.

After awhile, some of the rote sayings and prayers begin to seep into my consciousness. Prayers like, "Dear God, please relieve me of the bondage of self." Probably mostly because it is a prayer that sounds borderline kinky, I can retain it better than some of the others, able to call it forward out of the dust when I'm feeling particularly crazy.

I grew up with another version of this prayer, likely one Mom picked up at the same 12-Step group. Her translation: "You need to help others if you want to be happy."

"Yeah yeah," I'd think, going along my merry way or wondering which shoes to wear, but as I get older I silently counter with: *If a person is experiencing psychic or emotional pain, how can she think of others?* Isn't that like asking someone who just stubbed a toe to listen up to your good, long tale about fishing? Is the mind actually capable of managing empathy or sympathy when it's caught up in a swirl of real or imagined pain?

For years, I'd assumed the answer was "No." But then I had kids. Kids, those lovely little beings who insist on caviar right as you're amputating your right arm with a kitchen knife to feed your inner sharks. Beings, in short, who are egocentric enough not to mind even two blinks whether Mommy is tired, or hung over, or lonely, pushing to the front of the line so they can get their gruel first, hottest, and *just* right. All others be damned.

If nothing else, caring for the daily needs of young children proves to me that I do have the capacity to meet the needs of others regardless of the sickly condition of my own little city-state of self.

My 12-Step program pushes this theory one rung higher up the evolutionary ladder of loving-kindness. According to the program, in order to ensure one's own sobriety, one has to, in rather short order, help another ailing alcoholic—someone with less sobriety than you. The theory goes that helping out shows us we're much healthier and more capable than we think we are.

And the darnedest thing happens as I start working with other alcoholics: it begins to work. If I start spiraling into the dung heap of self-pity or romantic fantasies about drinking, I can easily distract myself by being helpful: doing dishes at meetings, introducing myself to newcomers, and eventually becoming a sponsor. Slowly, I start suspending my disbelief about my ability to be whole and helpful, just long enough to see myself being whole and helpful. A "Look! There's a pretty red bird!" strategy for those inclined to existential angst.

I can't speak for others, but for me, at roughly 10 months sober, I find it helpful to get more involved with the group and to start caring about others deeply. Getting involved turns out to be much less egocentric than "helping" or "saving." Rubber gloves prove much

Mommy Doesn't Drink Here Anymore

more helpful than a fancy red cape. Doing my part rather than being the savior, which is something quite new and different.

By going to meetings every day and listening to the tales of heartache, divorce, abuse, depression, illness, job loss, and the like, I come to prefer others' problems to my own. And even though we're encouraged to "live in the solution," it is incredibly inspiring to see people overcome hardships without taking a drink. Life is unimaginably hard for many people. Knowing that intellectually is one thing. Becoming connected to a fellowship of people who talk openly and honestly about these things is immensely freeing. I'm afraid it has spoiled me for civilian (non-recovering-alcoholic) company almost completely.

I get to put this theory to the test later in the summer, when Jack invites me to come along to an afternoon party and dinner for two of his best friends, Jed and Lane. Lane was recently diagnosed with terminal cancer, so this event is a good-bye of sorts.

In the old days, I'd meet any new situation or event with the cheerful thought that at least I could soften the whole experience with the cushion of many drinks. I'd have brought two bottles of my favorite white and hidden them well down at the bottom of the cooler so no one would drink them but me. I'd need at least two bottles for the afternoon event. And then for the dinner I would be able to try a new wine. Most people don't drink white wine, so I usually don't have much competition for the bottle. Supply and competition were two central themes of my drinking days.

Now that I'm sober, it feels like I have no protection against such a tragic event as a "Good-bye I'm dying soon from cancer" dinner. I worry and fret and then decide to go ahead and go along anyway. It means a lot to Jack that I attend the afternoon and evening events, and I've wanted to meet his friend Lane for some time now.

We arrive at a house in Edmonds on a sunny afternoon, and people are already gathering in the front yard, sharing delicious food and talking. I'm wearing heels and a pretty necklace as if these are protecting talismans and this is a den of sorrows. I see Lane and greet him and say "Hello." He looks healthy to me. But later he explains his situation. There is a group of women standing in the yard in various versions of skirts, pants, and dresses, but as I look around I see different states of concentration and emotion, ranging from concern to sweet oblivion to understanding and kindness.

Lane is explaining his cancer. "I had a spot removed six years ago, and now it's spread. It's in my lungs and other organs. I could have chosen to fight it, but then the treatment would have likely killed me anyway, and what quality of life would I have had?"

His determined openness and optimism are a relief. We ask a few questions, and then someone asks him how he's managing his pain. "I take Percocet and tried a pain patch but it was too strong." Apparently

Mommy Doesn't Drink Here Anymore

some teenagers have died by overdosing on the pain patch. According to Lane, they lick the patch looking for a high and then drop dead.

Later that afternoon, Jed is talking about the cruise he and Lane just took around the Mediterranean. They had fun, and Lane was healthy through the whole trip. When they returned, he had some pain and had to go to the emergency room, so it's looking like this trip to Europe was well timed, a moment of relief for Lane's last days on Earth. I look at Lane, look around at the others with their drinks in hand. The tragedy is like a chain around my ankle. Can the world still be a good place if someone so obviously lovely and caring and wonderful is so sick?

We finish visiting and then head back to our hotel room and get ready for dinner, which is at an Asian fusion restaurant in downtown Seattle. I'm nervous as hell and twitchy, a smidge beyond the reach of the Serenity Prayer, the prayer many 12-Steppers turn to in times of trouble. My version goes something like this:

God, grant me the serenity
God I hope everyone doesn't drink. Please let someone there be sober.
To accept the things I cannot change,
God, please heal Lane. Please let him live!
The courage to change the things I can,
How will Jed live without him? How will he survive this loss?
And the wisdom to know the difference.

At least I can still swear and drink coffee.

And at least I can wear pretty shoes. Switching between despair and fear and small things that make me smile is one of the bigger gifts of sobriety. I no longer get stuck worrying about the upcoming dinner. I stay there for a while, and then I focus on the Serenity Prayer, and then the sunny day, and then the dress my sweet daughter bought me for my birthday. In this way, I'm in a better head space more of the time.

As we arrive at the restaurant, Jack and I spot our group waiting in the bar. Since I haven't been inside a bar for ten months, I feel like shrieking, "Hi. I'm Rachael and I'm an alcoholic. And I cannot be trusted around alcohol!" Even though we're not supposed to do things like that. At least they could let me wear a "Beware: Alcoholic Within" T-shirt. Thankfully, as we walk in Jed and Lane announce, "Looks like we're all here so let's just get seated," and the hostess walks us to the main part of the restaurant.

As usual, I play the before-and-after movie.

Before Sobriety:

Yay! An opportunity to drink! Have babysitter, will party!

After Sobriety:

Any other sober peeps around this place? If I have another Diet Coke, will I have trouble falling asleep tonight? What if all I can do is cry?

We take our seats, and a woman I used to drink with sits down next to me. I immediately hop up like my seat is burning my high bottom and move to the other side of the table, explaining that I need to speak with Jed since I hardly ever get the chance. It is rude of me, and I can see that I've hurt her feelings. Here's what my sponsor would say about this situation: "Well, at least you didn't drink." This is either a miracle of forgiveness or a continual excuse for subpar behavior. I can't decide.

The guy next to me orders a rhubarb soda. I try not to gape and speak in a very loud, special voice when I say, "Does that have alcohol in it?!"

"Nope," he says, smiling.

He's happy he's not drinking! I bet he's in the program too! I bet he and I will talk through the evening, swapping "last drunk" stories. Maybe I'll finally have a gay best friend! This is going to be great!

"Are you sober?" I ask hopefully, like a kid asking if that present is for her.

"No. Just the designated driver."

I am so disappointed by his answer, I mutter a wan conversation starter: "Well, I'm having a Diet Coke," which is almost as riveting as "Hey! Want to see my rash?"

He nods politely, but I notice his eyes getting bigger as he searches his brain for the appropriate response. "Well, good. I like Diet Coke too."

"It sure is delicious," I say again as I kick Jack under the table, trying to spell out high-heel Morse Code for "H-E-L-P!" Lucky for Rhubarb Soda Guy, someone else interrupts our tête-à-tête.

Throughout the evening, I can't help watching Lane across the table, searching for signs of pain or discomfort. Instead, he looks healthy, happy, and fit. He's absolutely adorable. It's surreal to watch the others downing the cocktails. No one here leaves half a glass of wine sitting untouched. No one here drinks fewer than three glasses of booze in that first hour. Impressive. Less than a year ago, this would have been my idea of hog heaven. But not now. Now I'm trying not to cry and beg the universe to save Lane, but it isn't much different than throwing a penny in a fountain.

At times like this, I sure miss my alkie pals. If this were a bunch of addicts or alcoholics, we'd be laughing loudly and toasting imminent death, rocking the truth and tragedy of the occasion. It would rule.

About an hour later, a hippie girl three seats to my right asks everyone to go around the table and share favorite memories. She's very sweet. I bet she'd enjoy meetings. People are laughing and sharing happy times, funny recollections. It's very moving. I tear up (my new hobby) and look around, hoping someone else is sobbing into her kerchief. Nope. Just me. The Diet Coke representative trying to pick up the childless gay Rhubarb Soda Guy with her impressive repartee: "Have you ever seen a baby's diaper when it is filled with poop like black tar?! It's really incredible!"

At some point, about three Diet Cokes in, I realize I'm on the downward slide toward the Ugly Crying Sober Place (UCSP). This is a very bad place to be, especially if one is sitting around a huge circular table with others having fun and clinking cocktail glasses, cackling wildly about "that one night we didn't get home until 2, no, 3! No, 4 A.M.!" Joy-kill doesn't begin to cover what happens in the UCSP. It involves sobbing, runny nose, and facial contortions from some horror flick and many, many drunk people wondering why Jack's wife is off her can.

I decide it's best for all involved if I excuse myself before my insides match my outsides. Jack is understanding and offers to walk me to the valet, who retrieves the car key just in the nick of time.

I know intellectually that all the nice people there won't think anything of me slipping away quietly, but I also know that without me, Rhubarb Soda Guy will probably be desperately lonely. I hope I'm not being selfish running away because I'm afraid to cry in public with people who like to drink. I drive back to the hotel room, eat a Snickers, and call my sponsor. So goes another day in Sober-land.

At least I have a very high bottom.

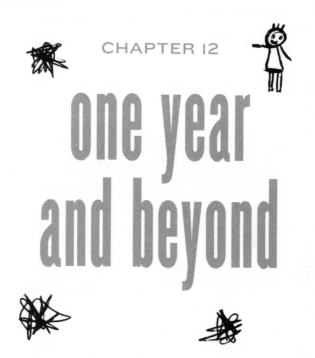

CHAPTER 12

one year and beyond

At one year sober, I am perfect. Dazzlingly beautiful and healthy, with a taut stomach and thighs, a tantric master, a person adored and cherished by all. I am humble and angelic and well.

I am Harriet the Spy, the precocious girl spy who grows into a centered scion of sober society. I spend a great deal of time with fantasies like the above, because in 12-Step groups, accomplishing that first year of sobriety is like running your first marathon, or giving birth to triplets with no pain medications, or appearing on *Oprah* for your world-renowned good deeds.

Completing one's first year of continuous sobriety is considered an important hurdle. The coin you receive reflects this and is weighty and official looking. In my group, the first-year coin is the first real metal coin you receive (the ones marking the various months are plastic). It is engraved with "To Thine Own Self Be True" and an official-looking Roman numeral I.

Early in sobriety, when I imagine taking my first-year coin, I think of a big party, a "This Is Your Life" gala, but with better shoes and more somber adoration. Reality exceeds my fiction-fed imaginings. The day I take my first-year coin, my friends and family sit in the room where I've come every day for a year, and the circle seems complete. Ted has moved to Oregon but he sends me a card and an email, and I carry him with me in my heart. My husband sits to my right with my sponsor in the row behind us.

When they ask if anyone is celebrating an annual birthday, I raise my hand, and everyone claps. I go up front where my sponsor stands with a coin, and she reviews what we've been through together this past year.

She gives me a coin that an old-timer has provided for the occasion. It's his from twenty years before, and as my sponsor says, "Has much good ju-ju."

I take my seat, and the chair asks me for a discussion topic. I suggest the First Step because that is the beginning and the end of it all for many of us. In the First Step, we admit we are powerless over alcohol and that our lives have become unmanageable. For me, as for others, I had no idea how unmanageable my life had become. Since I wasn't (yet) living under a bridge or incarcerated or ordered to meetings by the courts, left by family and friends because of my dissipation, I thought everything was fine.

Now I see things differently. My misery, fueled by alcoholism, was getting worse with each drink. My family was suffering, my loved ones in pain. Inured to their struggles, I kept worshiping alcohol and putting it first. Despite claims to the contrary, I put alcohol before my children, my marriage, my well-being, and I was only steps from complete breakdown.

A year later, I see these things through the lens of recovery. I realize my first step began the day I called my brother Jimmy and shared the sneaking suspicion that alcohol was morphing from an escape to a crutch to an addiction. That was my beginning. And the growing belief that my misery was a choice and that I could choose something different. Since that day, after all the withdrawal and tears and self-pity cleared up enough for me to see straight and look around, I chose the 12-Step program with the sayings and the advice and the people whose chilling stories were bellwethers of the inevitable end faced by alcoholics who don't find help soon enough: car crashes, children removed by social services, divorces, death, illness, mental breakdown, and every horrid possibility.

Against this gloomy backdrop, I began hearing what happens on the other side. People learn to laugh again. They heal their families, are reunited with children and parents and spouses, and can walk through suffering without the aid of alcohol or drugs or escapism. Never in my life have I met so many people whom I admire for their courage in the face of destruction—people who pick themselves up, make their way into a meeting, and learn to reach out for help, despite their pride and public image. In the rooms of this 12-Step program, I've met my heroes.

And then there's my marriage. Happiness in marriage, as in life, is like an oiled pig: difficult to chase down, impossible to conjure or command. I know. I've tried. But sex, drinking, religion, work, and even children haven't brought me the holy grail of joy. This year of sobriety is the closest I've come to happy and serene since I was a kid living in the cozy house by the woods. On the other hand, here I am nearly one year sober, and I still vacillate between aspiring

Mommy Doesn't Drink Here Anymore

Buddha and Joan Jett with a migraine. Luckily, at times like these, one of the 12-Step program sayings is apropos: *We seek after progress, not perfection.* And this saying should be emblazoned on the top right corner of my living room wall, probably in neon and with two additional words added: *in marriage.* When it comes to marriage, I still think everyone else is in college and I'm in pre-K playing with paste and requiring four special assistants. Marriage is my Black Box, a mystery I still don't understand. And yet, whatever hope there is to have, I try to hang on to it one day at a time. There is more laughter now in our house, more fun, more relaxing family time. Mommy and Daddy aren't such dullards and miserable sons of biscuits any longer. And lest this seem like damning through faint praise, I'll also say this: I looked over at Jack the other day, noticed his handsome face, and smiled.

At the close of book-study meetings, we read "The Promises," a list of possibilities for those who can stop drinking a day at a time. Early in sobriety, they seem unimaginably glorious, but as time goes on they seem possible. "The Promises" state that if we work hard and stay close to the program, we'll find happiness and freedom, peace and security, and will intuitively understand what to do when we face challenging situations. In short, we'll be spiritually centered and able to meet "calamity with serenity."

In the beginning, we are encouraged to make a list of things we'd like to see happen in our lives. The idea is that no matter what you write down, after a few years your life will be unrecognizable to you, better than anything you can imagine. We aren't promised sweet little convertibles, interviews with Oprah, dates with Balthazar Getty, or free trips to London and Paris. But we are promised that we will receive graces of the spirit beyond our wildest dreams (if we work for them).

Very early on, I'm not sure I could have been particularly articulate on the topic of deeply held dreams and desires, mostly because I didn't know what the hell I wanted. I just knew I didn't want the life I had. But now, one year sober, I'm like an eight-year-old planning a trip to the mall to see Santa with a list prepared two weeks in advance, sorted by type, color, and price.

At one year sober, my list goes something like this:

1. To feel happy and content and serene more often than not
2. To do work I love and enjoy
3. To have good health
4. To have a primary relationship that is romantic, lustful, laughter filled, and adventurous
5. To have happy, healthy, secure, and innocent children
6. To have a Democrat (any Democrat!) in the White House
7. To enjoy close friendships and fellowship
8. To laugh hard and often

Mommy Doesn't Drink Here Anymore

9. To have fun
10. For people who need it to find the program and give up the hooch, so they can join me at the crazy Diet Coke table at holiday dinners.

. . . And to always look thirty-five.

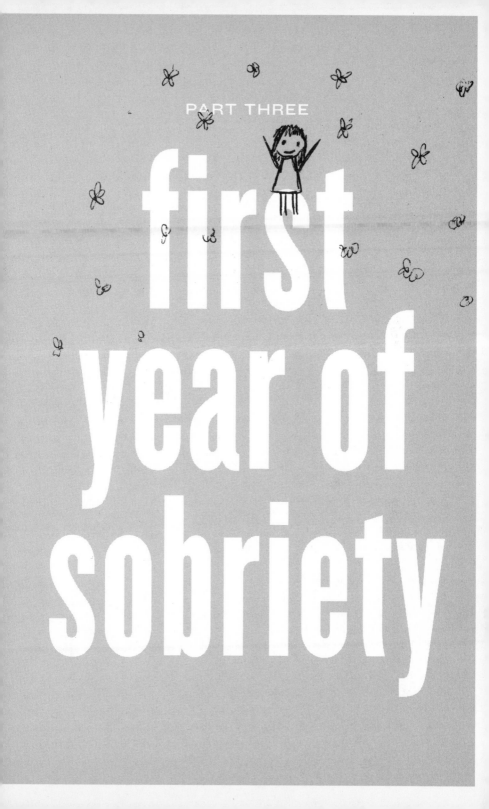

PART THREE

first
year of
sobriety

CHAPTER 13

alternatives
to the cocktail
playdate

I love the concept of the cocktail playdate. It represents parents carving out an adult space, a tunnel running underneath the river of messy toys and screaming progeny. Parents are people who need more support, more naps, and far more loving-kindness than they often get. The cocktail playdate is a funny description of an effort to create an intersection between kids and adults that doesn't completely wave the white flag and surrender the tanker to the enemy. "It's okay, honey, Mommy will just eat your crusts."

So many spaces and times are completely overrun and no longer adult-friendly, never mind kid-friendly. Babysitters require background checks, public education is going downhill fast, and studies come out daily that indicate how we're the wet noodle arm failing to protect our children from the car crash of life. Who wouldn't drink under these circumstances? So the cocktail playdate is definitely a step in the right direction.

Except for people who have a problem with alcohol.

Ultimately, all I gave myself in terms of rest and self-care was wine. Not extra sleep, not healthy food or exercise, not anything real or deep for myself, not time with girlfriends, or time to think. Just wine. That's it.

And wine, as it turns out, a perfectly reasonable rallying cry of freedom for plenty of normal drinkers, was a self-serving bitch to me. A real asshole. So for me, one of the first exercises was to find ways to chuck the bottle in favor of things that served the real purpose of a cocktail playdate. Time to myself or with friends that didn't revolve around diapers or dishes or laundry or bill paying. Time to have fun and be carefree and laugh out loud.

I love what it means to have time with other parents when the focus isn't always about the children. It's really the symbolism of drinking that I miss now more than the actual booze. So finding an alternative is crucial, an acceptable substitute that is more than club soda in a tall cool glass, something deeper.

Leaving aside the parental relief that would be provided by universalized health care, high-quality state-sponsored child care, and grannies-for-hire, here are some things that have helped me find time for myself. Some alternatives to the cocktail playdate:

- Returning to things I used to enjoy before I became Mistress of the Wine Bottle: reading, writing, staring at the rain, pretending to be prim and proper.
- Going to meetings: At first I went because I had to. Now I go because it's fun.
- Napping: Ditch the guilt and do it. It's fabulous.
- Cooking: If I can learn to think cooking is relaxing, anyone can.
- Swearing: It's like a mini-vacation from Mommy Mouth. Swearing rules! Of course if you're getting together with kids, bring a kerchief into which you can whisper your cursing.
- Scrapbooking: Just kidding. I still hate scrapbooking and the bad wind it blew in on.

- ⭐ Sober girl get-togethers: Honestly, I can't think of anything more fun these days than hanging out with my sober girlfriends and laughing it up about this or that. We went roller-skating the other week, and I can't remember the last time I smiled from my toes to my head. If I'd been in a dark cave, I'd have lit up the place.
- ⭐ Going on a bike ride with the kiddies.
- ⭐ Baking, which is much, much better when one is sober and centered. Your kids will love it!
- ⭐ Neighborhood sober get-togethers: Much like the get-togethers you had when you were drinking, except now everyone else won't leave early and whisper about your bizarre behavior.
- ⭐ Kids' movies/Parent's poker: Put the kids in front of a movie so the 'rents can play cards.

The thing about drinking in order to have fun is that after awhile, it takes more and more drinks to get to that sweet spot. It becomes more about managing the hangover and the stress, more about killing the pain and filling up empty space, and less like a hootin' hollerin' great time. It's like gorging on cotton candy when what you really need is steak (or an eggplant, if you're vegetarian). Drinking is many things, but soul satisfying it isn't, at least not for people like me.

In the end, I turned to alcohol as a proxy and a quick fix for deeper troubles. Over time, I've found richer ways of being fulfilled and rejuvenated, some of which are unpublishable here. Still, even my old drinking self would approve of some of the goals I've set for my forty-first birthday—like jumping out of an airplane (one hopes with parachute), and taking a road trip with my best girlfriends down Highway 101 along the California coast, or traveling to Paris and London sober.

how to get help

No one but you can decide whether you have a problem with drugs or alcohol. Only you, in your secret heart, hear the whispering voices of doom in the morning when you first wake up and realize, again, that you had more to drink than you'd planned. Or perhaps you already know but have given up all hope of ever recovering. Maybe you're in the "fuck it" stage of your life.

Maybe the jobs, cars, family members are gone and you're all alone. Maybe you wonder whether your life is worth living anymore, or why you feel so empty and used up inside.

No matter. Wherever you are is right where you're supposed to be (annoying, isn't it?). Come as you are. You can be angry, dirty, scared, or jubilant. You can think 12-Step groups are the occult. Just show up, and the people will accept and love you.

Don't believe me? Give it a try. I double-dog dare you.

do you have a problem with alcohol?

There is a quiz people pass around in 12-Step groups that helps us figure out if we have a problem with alcohol, but it can apply to many things: food, sex, pain medication, anger, or anything we use to manage our lives or kill the pain.

Answer Yes or No to the following questions.

1. Have you ever tried unsuccessfully to give up alcohol?
2. Have others expressed concern about your drinking and using?
3. Have you ever employed various methods of cutting back your alcohol (including switching drinks, only drinking on weekends, or after 7 P.M., or never in the morning)?
4. Have you ever had a drink before noon?
5. Do you wonder why you don't drink like other people?
6. Have you had any alcohol-related trouble in the past year (DUIs, court orders, jobs lost)?
7. Has your drinking caused any problems with your family or in your home life?
8. Do you ever have a few drinks before an event because you are worried there won't be enough there?

9. Do you frequently have difficulty stopping at just one drink?
10. Have you ever missed work or school because of a hangover?
11. Do you have trouble remembering what happens after a certain number of drinks?
12. Have you wondered if your life might be better without alcohol?

If you answered "Yes" four or more times, *you* might have a problem with alcohol. I took this quiz a few times myself in secret and made sure not to answer "Yes" more than three times. But after awhile, I went back and answered the questions truthfully. I said "Yes" to nearly every one.

Even so, let me be absolutely clear on this point: Whether you have a problem with alcohol is between you and you. Only you can decide at what point you might need or want help. The nice thing about most 12-Step groups is that you're always welcome to check them out, no strings attached. There is no need to commit, sign a contract, or say anything out loud.

other resources

Here are some helpful resources, even if you're pretty sure *the other guy's* the one who needs help:

Alcoholics Anonymous
Web site: *www.aa.org*.
Click on your state to find the number of your state general service office.
Phone: AA World Service (212) 870-3400

Narcotics Anonymous
Web site: *www.na.org*
Phone: NA World Service (818) 773-9999

about the author

Rachael Brownell grew up and around Seattle, Washington, the middle girl between two loving but very odd brothers. An avowed tomboy until age 33, Rachael discovered motherhood and gender as biological destiny simultaneously. She is a former non-profit executive, an active writer, fundraiser, mother of three and a recovering alcoholic. She has written for *Imperfect Parent* and *Babble* and is currently the managing editor of Super Eco, Crowd Fusions' green living site. Rachael lives with her family in Northwest Washington State.

to our readers

Conari Press, an imprint of Red Wheel/Weiser, publishes books on topics ranging from spirituality, personal growth, and relationships to women's issues, parenting, and social issues. Our mission is to publish quality books that will make a difference in people's lives—how we feel about ourselves and how we relate to one another. We value integrity, compassion, and receptivity, both in the books we publish and in the way we do business.

Our readers are our most important resource, and we value your input, suggestions, and ideas about what you would like to see published. Please feel free to contact us, to request our latest book catalog, or to be added to our mailing list.

Conari Press
An imprint of Red Wheel/Weiser, LLC
500 Third Street, Suite 230
San Francisco, CA 94107
www.redwheelweiser.com